Wakefield Press

Finding Santana

Melbourne-born Jill Jolliffe began her career as a journalist in 1975 covering the Indonesian takeover of Portuguese Timor for Reuters newsagency.

Between 1978 and 1998 she was based in Portugal, freelancing for a range of media companies, including the *Guardian*, the *Sunday Times*, the *Eastern Express*, the BBC, the *Age* and *The Christian Science Monitor*. During this time she covered news, political and cultural events in Portugal, Spain, Angola, Mozambique, Western Sahara, Macau, China and south-east Asia. She returned to Australia in 1999 and travelled to East Timor to cover the withdrawal of Indonesian troops after a 24-year occupation.

In 2004 Jill Jolliffe was granted the Eric Dark Fellowship by Varuna, the Writer's House, to complete the manuscript of *Finding Santana*.

With a group of Timorese former political prisoners, in 2005 she founded The Living Memory Project, a movement dedicated to creating a video archive based on testimony of freed prisoners and torture survivors.

In 2006 she was named Journalist of the Year by Yale University's *Global* magazine for her writing on justice and human rights issues.

Jill Jolliffe continues to work as a journalist and is writing her autobiography as a PhD with Flinders University.

By the same author

East Timor: Nationalism and Colonialism

Timor, Terra Sangrenta [Timor: The Killing Fields]

Aviz: A Lisbon Story

Depois das Lagrimas [After the Tears], ed.

Cover-up

Balibo

Finding Santana

Jill Jolliffe

Wakefield
Press

Wakefield Press
1 The Parade West
Kent Town
South Australia 5067
www.wakefieldpress.com.au

First published 2010

Cover design by Mark Thomas
Typeset by Wakefield Press
Printed and bound by Hyde Park Press, Adelaide

National Library of Australia Cataloguing-in-Publication entry

Author:	Jolliffe, Jill.
Title:	Finding Santana/Jill Jolliffe.
ISBN:	978 1 86254 925 8 (pbk.).
Subjects:	Sanatana, Nino Konis – Interviews.
	Jolliffe, Jill – Diaries.
	Forbes, Anna.
	Guerrillas – Timor-Leste.
	Military intelligence – Indonesia – History.
	Timor-Leste – History – 20th century.
Dewey Number:	355.0218095987

This book was written with the assistance of an Eric Dark Fellowship from Varuna, The Writers' House

Publication of this book was assisted by the Commonwealth Government through the Australia Council, its arts funding and advisory body.

Contents

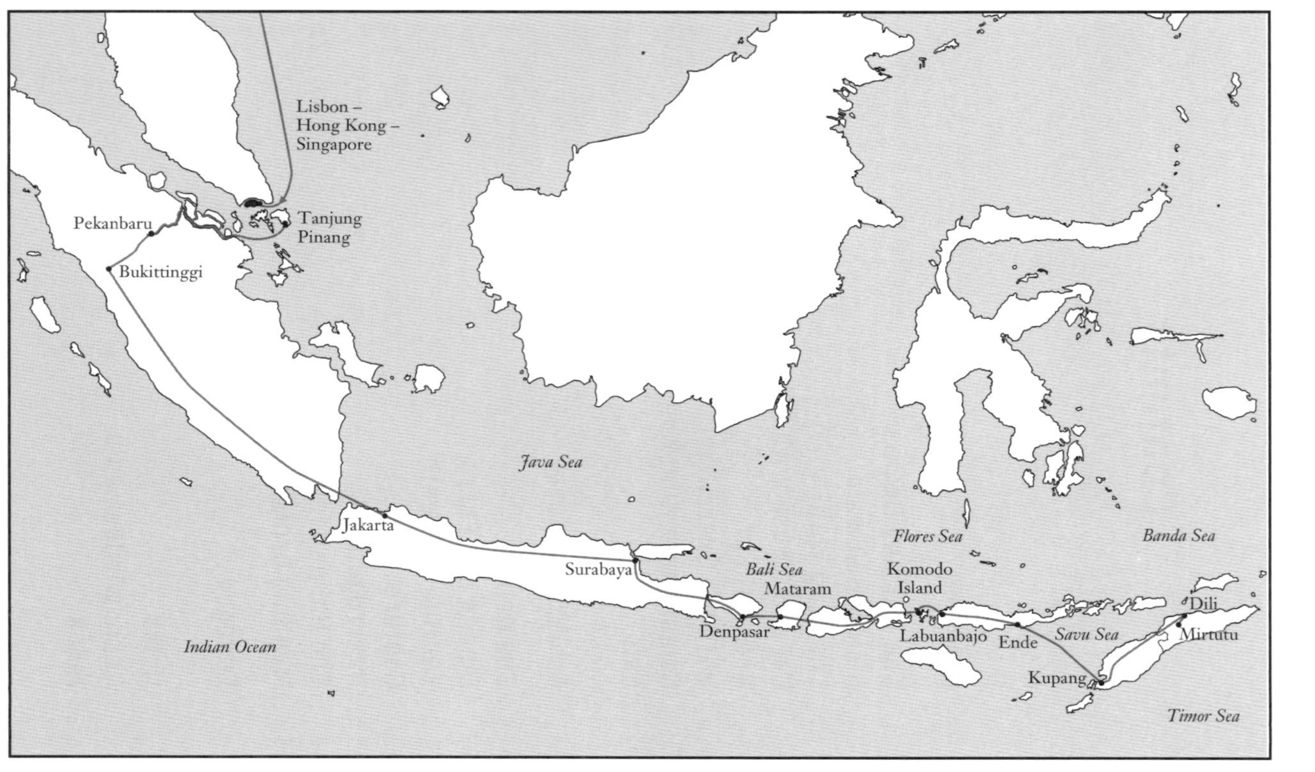

Indonesian archipelago and East Timor, showing the route taken by the author on her first visit to Nino Konis Santana in mid-1994

Book I

Contact

Prologue

So'e, 3 August 1994

By the noodle stall at the end of Jalan Kartini, F.F.'s face loomed up out of the dusk. He was in a rage, a condition I had never seen him in before. 'Where have you been? Why didn't you turn up? I've been waiting for days!' he hissed. Despite his wrath, I was terribly glad to see him.

It took some time to quieten him down by explaining what had happened. Tommy, my dear and faithful companion in misadventure, stood at my side, nodding agreement with my version. There are hundreds, if not thousands, of streets in Indonesia called after the feminist hero Kartini, and so there was a Jalan Kartini in Kupang, capital of West Timor, just as there was in So'e, the next town down the road in the direction of the East Timor border. When Tommy and I had been unable to meet in Kupang because of constant harassment by the secret police, we decided to hide out in So'e until F.F. arrived to organise the next phase of the journey and to bring me more of the money I had sent to his account from Australia.

Under the system I used with the East Timorese resistance operatives, whenever I moved from one place to another Tommy or I would ring the youthful Zely in Jakarta, who acted as a sort of telephone anchorman. We would tell him where I was and he would then tell F.F. when he rang in. Zely had failed to absorb the fact that we were in Jalan Kartini, *So'e*, and not in Jalan Kartini, *Kupang*, which is where F.F. had been waiting for us. When Tommy discovered what had happened, he came as close to cursing at Zely on the telephone as a good Timorese Catholic can. 'The bonehead! I'm going to kill him, I'm going to kill him!' he inveighed when he came back.

This misunderstanding had caused us serious anguish. For the past week Tommy and I had been sharing a cockroach-infested room costing around 50c a night in the flophouse of Andre, a local eccentric. Its garden was studded with Roman-style plaster statues painted in garish colours and he had built a new guest wing in the shape of the *Johannes*, a frigate Britain's Margaret Thatcher had sold to the Indonesian navy at cut-price after the Falklands war. (Because his middle name was Johannes, he felt a special affinity with the vessel and, indeed, had been invited on board for its inaugural voyage in this new theatre of war.) The aesthetic originality of our lodgings could not, however, compensate for the fact that we were living on little more than a plate of noodles a day and whatever bananas or mangoes we could get at the market. In the past few days we had trudged through the market several times trying to sell my watch. I was too proud to present the image of an Australian hippy begging in Asia, so I asked Tommy to pretend it was his. The stallholders stared knowingly at the white strip on my arm, unmarked by the sun.

That had failed, so Tommy had used some of our last rupiahs to travel back to Kupang and try to find F.F. He was gone for two days and I was almost desperate when he returned. Stranded and penniless, I was in danger of coming to police attention. If they picked me up and looked at the name on my passport I was doomed. In my diary I wrote bitter words against both him and F.F., which I regretted when he returned and told me he'd had to sleep in the street because he couldn't afford even the cheapest room in the city.

F.F.'s anger was a minor matter after the indignities we had suffered. The problem was that we had lost another one of the precious eight weeks allowed on my tourist visa. Renewing it within the borders of Indonesia was out of the question because it would reveal my illegal status, and I now had only a fortnight to enter East Timor, cross Indonesian lines, interview guerrilla commander Nino Konis Santana in the mountains and return along the archipelago to Sumatra for a boat back to Singapore. I had waited weeks hidden in a room in the backpackers' quarter of Jakarta for Santana's authorisation to proceed. Then there had been a false start when F.F., Tommy and I had booked a 30-hour bus journey to Bali but had to get off the bus and separate after we were questioned by a passenger who had heard us speaking Portuguese. He turned out to be a military judge returning to his post in Dili, with two other officers. We waited till the bus stopped for a coffee break in Surabaya, grabbed our bags and fled. The new plan involved separating, with F.F. returning to Jakarta and Tommy travelling in the bus behind me until we all met up again in Kupang, but we had lost valuable time. The latest disaster had not helped.

After he accepted our explanations, F.F. unveiled the next phase of the operation. Twilight had given way to night as we stood beside the highway leading to East Timor, so I was glad he couldn't see the blood drain from my face as he asked, 'Can you cross the border alone?' I had taken comfort from the thought that after Jakarta I would have a resistance escort all the way, but now I had to face a different reality. Tommy muttered embarrassedly, 'If you get caught you'll just be deported, but if I get caught with you I'll do ten years in Cipinang prison.' 'I'll be travelling behind,' he added in compensation. I'd come so far, and knew I couldn't turn back now after all the work that had been done. I knew too that his assessment was correct and that he had every right to pull out, but I would have liked to have known this intention earlier. I murmured agreement.

The plan was to catch a bus into Suai, East Timor's south coast border town, after changing at Atambua, last major town on the West Timorese side. F.F. produced a letter to

Father Hilário Madeira, the parish priest, asking him to drive me into the mountains immediately when I arrived there. I tucked it in my pocket, we embraced, and I stepped apprehensively into the night bus crammed with passengers, chickens and goats. I watched the familiar silhouettes of my two friends fade into the distance. Nineteen years after leaving East Timor, I was finally returning.

1
The Journey Begins

Lisbon to Tanjung Pinang, 30 April – 19 June 1994

The journey had begun a couple of months earlier from Lisbon, where I had been based as a foreign correspondent since 1978.

First experience of East Timor had been gained as a novice reporter for Reuters newsagency in September 1975, observing the early phases of the Indonesian invasion. Three months of intensive reporting had been followed by evacuation by the International Committee of the Red Cross on 4 December. In the interim five colleagues, later known as the Balibo Five, had been shot in cold blood by Indonesian special forces in a cross-border sweep on 16 October.

As all other journalists were leaving, freelancer Roger East took the brave decision to remain and try to report the invasion. He was executed publicly four days later during the paratroop landing on Dili. Thousands of Timorese died along with East, but the repercussions in both cases were short-lived. The world slipped into forgetfulness.

In early 1976 the Indonesian government informed relevant Australian media companies that three of their journalists were henceforth banned from travelling to Indonesia or East Timor. I was one of them. The others were Michael Richardson of Melbourne's *Age* newspaper, who had been evacuated at the same time, and Bruce Wilson of the Melbourne *Herald*, who had reported on Jakarta's pre-invasion military operations from Kupang.

With the death of East and the announcement of these banning orders, the territory had been sealed off from the world. With rare exceptions, the information blockade imposed then still prevailed in 1994. Behind it, killings, imprisonments and torture continued unchecked, although superficial aspects of Indonesian rule changed constantly, depending on whether the carrot or the stick was being employed to persuade the population to accept annexation.

One motive for moving to Portugal from my native Australia had been to seek credible information about the situation since the invasion. By 1978 the only refugees to have escaped were in Lisbon, after being air-lifted from camps in Atambua under a 1976 agreement between the Indonesian and Portuguese governments. Around 2000 lived in a muddy encampment at Vale do Jamor, just outside the Portuguese capital. After a flurry of publicity when they first arrived, the refugees had been forgotten, apart from a brief peak of interest around 1979 when they were visited by Princess Grace of Monaco, otherwise known as film star Grace Kelly, who donated funds for their schooling and health care. They lived crowded together in shacks and army tents, each family's quarters marked out by blankets hanging from the ceiling, with the children and old folk subject to respiratory illnesses in the bitter Lisbon winter. But they were united by deep cultural ties, homesickness and knowledge of the danger of systematic extermination their people faced.

Private letters that Timorese smuggled out of the territory to family members in Lisbon were heart-rending, but valuable in documenting the course of the war. They told of summary executions, arbitrary imprisonments and torture, and mass deaths in the countryside from bombardment, starvation and disease. They also spoke of an organised resistance army still fighting in the mountains.

The world press was not listening to these claims. Instead the view from Jakarta prevailed: that the East Timorese had been joyfully 'reunited' with their Indonesian brothers in December 1975 and there was no resistance to rule from Jakarta. If I could access the territory to chart human rights violations and talk to Timorese leaders, I could contribute to changing the world's perception of the issue.

From the time I arrived in Portugal I had been anxious to return to East Timor as soon as possible to try and interview those guerrilla fighters. After all, there was only so much that could be written using refugee sources. Some nationalist leaders were living in exile in Portugal, and it had seemed the best place from which to plan such a venture. However, years passed and the project was still unrealised.

During the long wait from my Lisbon base I made a conscious effort to accumulate further experience in combat zones and improve composure under fire.

Coverage from Timor in 1975 had involved a drubbing from mortar shells at Mota Ain, strafing by a B26 bomber at Atabae and a close encounter with a bow-and-arrow in untamed Lete-foho). In 1982 I reported on fighting between Polisario Front guerrillas and Moroccan troops in the Western Sahara, and in 1988 had an adrenaline-drenched experience when caught in a South African artillery attack, during Angola's battle of Cuito Cuanavale.

But these were only training runs for return to East Timor. By the early 1990s three other journalists had run the Indonesian blockade. There was *Paris-Match* photographer Denis Reichle in 1976, Australian trade unionist Robert Domm in 1990 (the first outsider to interview commander Xanana Gusmão, for the Australian Broadcasting Corporation's 'Background Briefing'), and Portugal's Mário Robalo, in 1991, who also interviewed Gusmão, for the Lisbon weekly *Expresso*.

Hopes of return were raised in 1991 by the planned visit of a delegation from the Portuguese parliament, brokered by the UN. As head of the foreign press association in Portugal, the foreign ministry asked me to select five international correspondents to accompany the parliamentarians. The Indonesian government was also assembling a team. After long negotiations our group included radio, television and newspaper reporters, covered most continents of the world and represented the English, Portuguese, Indonesian and French-speaking media. The group had been conceived as a team in the deepest sense, and we were interdependent in our combined skills. The Indonesian government had rejected Pascal Mallet, the Jakarta bureau chief of Agence France-Presse, so he was included in the Portuguese selection.

The story of that ill-fated project offers material for a book in itself. The Timorese believed it was their salvation, an opening to the democratic world after years of repression. They planned massive demonstrations to coincide with the delegation's arrival, but it was never to be. The 1976 Indonesian ban remained in place and although the UN terms stipulated that there should be no vetoes of the journalists chosen, Jakarta insisted on my exclusion. Foreign minister Ali Alatas said such a presence was unthinkable, describing me as 'a friend of FRETILIN', East Timor's leading nationalist party. The parliamentarians argued that they would travel only when the ban on me was lifted. Indonesia refused, and the mission collapsed.

Tension in Dili was running high and in following days frustrated students took to the streets. For the first time, they displayed banners of Gusmão and shouted independence slogans. As they entered Santa Cruz cemetery they were shot down in cold blood by Indonesian soldiers. Those who survived the first rounds of semi-automatic fire were finished off with bayonets.

The killings were filmed and photographed by a group of human rights activists and journalists who had been infiltrated into the territory by Timorese leaders abroad to await the parliamentarians. The seductive presence of television cameras had encouraged the disappointed demonstrators to take prematurely to the streets.

Around 80 East Timorese died, along with Kamal Bamadhaj, an activist from the University of New South Wales. But the difference between this massacre and many others that had preceded it was that this one had been filmed. The images shocked the world and changed perceptions of East Timor's suffering.

A year later Gusmão was captured in Dili. He was put on trial and imprisoned in Jakarta's Cipinang jail for life, a sentence reduced to 20 years after international outcry. Two other prominent guerrillas, Mau Huno and Ma' Hodu, succeeded him in turn as leader, before also being captured by the Indonesian army. By 1994 Nino Konis Santana, a native of the eastern Tutuala district, was leading the military struggle.

In the wake of these events, Timorese friends in Lisbon pressed me not to wait any longer, or to remain dependent on their leaders abroad. They would secure the resistance contacts I needed. 'You can do it, Jill, if you avoid plane travel, cross the border by boat and stick to land and sea routes,' they asserted. Preparations began.

The big problem was Ali Alatas's blacklist. Timorese taken in for questioning had told of seeing my photo displayed inside police and military posts in Indonesia. A bid to buy a fake passport in another name involved a forger from a feudal-era village in northern Portugal. João das Mentiras—'John the Liar'—could have stepped out of the pages of Chaucer. He was a gross, unwashed figure who insisted on conducting business in a stockyard containing his prize fighting steer. 'You won't get a better passport than my American model,' he boasted, as it snorted and pawed the ground, '—people enter New York weekly on it.' The price was exorbitant and the quality uncertain. The risk of being arrested for travelling on a forged passport at London's

Heathrow airport, long before coming anywhere close to Indonesia, was too great to contemplate.

The only solution was the one urged by the Timorese: to count on the low standards of Indonesian monitoring at obscure border posts that did not have computers, and slip into the country that way. They recommended the much-frequented ferry from Singapore to Batam Island, favoured by weekend golfers.

Using this route, the journey would involve travelling around 3000 km across the Indonesian archipelago by land and sea. Batam is one of Indonesia's Riau islands, stepping-stones between Singapore and Sumatra. From Sumatra, travel would be eastward to the central island of Java, and then to the Lesser Sunda group: through Bali, Lombok, Sumbawa and Flores to Timor, the final goal.

It promised to be an exciting journey, not just because it was illegal and therefore dangerous. Contrary to foreign minister Alatas's claims, I had never been anti-Indonesian. While fearing and disliking the military, I yearned for real contact with Indonesians and their culture, and was impatient to begin travelling and, along the way, to discover how they lived and what they thought.

Fitness was a concern. Nineteen years had gone by since I had first marched with Timorese guerrillas. They could tread precarious jungle trails with the speed and ease of mountain goats, and I had problems keeping up even then. There is an unspoken rule that a journalist should not undertake dangerous assignments unless fit enough to run to save his or her life, literally. This was probably no longer a realistic expectation, but a personal program to improve general fitness seemed a reasonable compromise.

The community in Lisbon maintained good contact with guerrillas in the East Timorese mountains, working through intermediary networks. These had a strong student component and operated mainly from Jakarta and Bali, relaying letters, emails and telephone messages to Dili, and thence to the mountains, using couriers to hand-carry these vital communications.

By the mid-1990s the resistance was divided into political factions, or at least its secondary layers were. The guerrilla leaders refused to be affected, closing ranks against their common enemy, the Indonesian army. So it was that among students in Portugal, Macau, Jakarta, Bali and Dili, there was a myriad of networks, many of which (usually the most vocal and radical-sounding) had been infiltrated by Indonesian intelligence agents. In some other cases there was evidence that individuals in mainstream resistance structures were double-dealing with the secret police.

In setting up contacts before departure, it was therefore necessary to proceed with the utmost caution. A 'clean' network was needed, avoiding contact with any individuals who might be slightly compromised, and there had to be rigorous secrecy in the planning.

In early 1994 exiled resistance veteran Rogério Lobato promised to set up a main contact. Later a Timorese who identified himself only as 'Natan', the Portuguese equivalent of Nathan, visited my Lisbon apartment.

Departure date was already planned because, by a stroke of luck, the press association had been offered a cut-price visit of ten days to the Chinese coastal enclave of Macau, Portugal's last colony, and this was to occur in May. It was half-way to Timor and would reduce costs enormously. The plan was to remain behind when my colleagues returned to Portugal, with the cover story of a reporting assignment around south-east Asia, excluding Timor because of my banned status. I had to learn to lie consistently and convincingly, even to friends.

Natan gave instructions on contacting the Timorese underground in Jakarta, who would then plan and assist onward travel to the mountains of their homeland. There was a telephone number to call on arrival and a rendezvous point at the entrance to the Monas monument in Jakarta's main park where a Timorese would approach me. Recognition would be from a book, the cover of which would be described to them in advance. We agreed on the Berlitz travel guide to Thailand, which had a pale blue cover with a photograph of Buddhist palaces decorated in gold leaf. He drilled me on the extreme danger of the situation—for me and my contacts—and the necessity of concealing plans from all other people. 'You must not speak of this to anyone else, repeat, anyone, from this moment on,' he stressed, 'or it could cost lives.' This agreed discipline created some problems. Going to East Timor to write newspaper stories and perhaps to film for television required discussion with editors beforehand, either to raise finance or enlist a camera operator. Some money had been set aside to pay for the basic travel, and living costs for a couple of months, but it was not a luxurious amount.

The Macau trip went ahead and I was sad to farewell my colleagues at the end of it. They were all good friends who I was unlikely to see for some time. Alexander Sloop, a reporter from UPI, had a knowing gleam in his eyes as we parted. 'Are you sure you're not going to East Timor?' he asked. 'You know I'm banned from there,' I replied, and we left it at that.

On the agenda after their departure was a complete image change and a new passport, both to be obtained in neighbouring Hong Kong.

Because of a row with the Portuguese government over East Timor, Australia had closed its embassy in Lisbon sometime before. It had never had representation in Macau but Australia had a High Commission in Hong Kong dealing with visa and passport matters. Unfortunately my passport was not yet full, so I couldn't invoke this reason for changing it. The alternative reason I concocted was not terribly credible, that as a journalist who needed to work in Angola, I could not return to that country because the current passport had the stamp of its neighbouring enemy Zaire in it, but it was the best I could think of.

At that time I wore my hair long, coloured with an auburn dye. A suburban Hong Kong hairdresser administered a severe short haircut and a dose of raven black dye. A search of the shops produced a pair of plain glass spectacles to be worn full-time (instead of glasses worn only for reading). The transformation was dramatic: all that was lacking were some fresh passport photos.

The Australian High Commission on a Saturday morning was a good time to apply, the consul being bleary-eyed from a long night out on the expatriate bar scene. There was a stark contrast between the photo in the old passport and that presented for the new—although there was no denying the second photo was of *me*. It was processed without a murmur and I emerged with a passport that still bore my name, had a photo not resembling my previous self and yet which matched my real appearance. Furthermore, it had no tell-tale Lisbon stamps in it. I caught the first plane to Singapore.

On Singapore's bustling wharf, I bought a ticket to Tanjung Pinang on Batam Island, from which there was a connecting ferry to Sumatra. In principle, Australian tourists were entitled to an eight-week visa on arrival. Despite the elaborate preparation, I was in a state of high anxiety as the boat cast off. I was still on Ali Alatas's blacklist, banned from entry for the previous 19 years because of articles about Indonesian military policy in East Timor. There had been enormous press publicity over the parliamentary mission. Even if there weren't computers, the passport would have to be read and stamped and might arouse suspicion.

These fears dissolved slightly as I idly read the ticket

while the boat plied on towards Indonesia and discovered the visa had been issued with it, before entering territorial waters. There it was, writ large: 'The Republic of Indonesia', followed by the words: 'Jill Jolliffe: Welcome to Indonesia'.

It was a brief respite. Soon the palm-fringed wooden pier at Tanjung Pinang came into view. My mouth went dry at the sight of uniformed figures awaiting the passengers under the fluttering red and white Indonesian flag.

The only Westerner on the small vessel, I hauled my luggage onshore as in a dream, fighting to dominate fear. I had forgotten that I would have to change the new glasses for reading glasses to fill in the immigration form, although I needed to have them on to match the photo. Somehow I went through the motions, achieving external calm, but could not control a visibly trembling hand while giving the passport over the counter. The officer read it slowly, extracting and keeping the immigration form. Then he stamped it, and politely handed it back. I was across the border.

2

Inside Indonesia

Sumatra to Java, 24 June – 9 July 1994

Indonesia in 1994 was a dictatorship under the sway of General Suharto, who had come to power as president in a bloody coup in 1965. Over half a million citizens died in the name of suppressing communism. He had deposed Sukarno, also a general, who led the independence struggle against the Dutch and founded the republican nation in 1949. There were now signs that the regime was entering into decay, with rumours of rifts among military officers. Indonesia had a parliament, but it was a rubber stamp for the military, so for now the iron grip of the army still prevailed.

There were three days to wait until the boat to Sumatra, which the *Lonely Planet* guide said took 36 hours between Tanjung Pinang and the Sumatran port of Pekanbaru, a voyage that it compared to Kurz's nightmare trip up the Congo river in Joseph Conrad's *Heart of Darkness.*

The *Lonely Planet* guides act as a travel bible for thousands of backpackers. Their value lies in the off-beat inside information they provide, and studying the volume on Indonesia was a good way to prepare for the problems I faced. It was not always reliable, but by reading its description of the next town along the way, it was possible to calculate the safest place to stay and estimate where the largest concentrations of backpackers might be. They could serve as protective cover—the more there were around, the better. I had decided on a new cover story for this phase of the trip—Jane Carlton, real estate agent from Sydney, travelling eastward to meet some friends in Bali. This was the lie to be told with total consistency, but never within sight of my passport.

In these days on the island I established a pattern of behaviour for the journey, knowing that success would only come with self-discipline, patience and wariness. I booked into a *losmen* with the standard basic bed, overhead fan and *mandi* and stayed inside except for a morning walk and forays to the marketplace or a nearby restaurant for meals. The routine involved killing time for days on end, which I did lying on the bed smoking *kreteks*, Indonesia's favourite clove cigarettes, watching the fan swish above, and listening to the BBC, a lifeline to the outer world.

I was concerned that a bit of paper, the immigration form, had remained at the wharf as a record of entry. What if they went over the slips more carefully afterwards, to check against a blacklist? Did the forms eventually go to Jakarta? It was not out of the question that they could later discover that I had crossed illegally, leading to arrest. The best option was to put as much distance as possible between me and the border, but I could go nowhere until the boat came.

In my nervousness I became accident-prone, slicing the top off a toe while trimming my nails, and later setting fire to the foam rubber mattress with ash from a *kretek*, an accident that I was able to conceal by rapid action and some intricate razor cuts to the scorched sheets, but which was to be repeated in another variation in my onward travels.

The day the ferry sailed I was the first to buy a ticket, for 'cabin' number 66. This consisted of a body-sized floor space covered in linoleum, with a ceiling about a metre high. It was possible to sit up but not to stand, although each area—marked out by wooden slats—had the saving grace of a porthole. It was a large vessel with various tiers of these cabins, into which the passengers inserted themselves like sardines in a tin; it probably carried around 200–250 people, a classical overcrowded Third World ferry. It was not clear whether it was seaworthy—only the voyage would tell—but it was certainly old.

The name Sumatra conjures up steamy jungles and rare species, such as the Sumatran tiger, the orang-utan and the two-horned rhinoceros. Since the mid-19th century when naturalist Alfred Russel Wallace visited, conservationists have been warning that land use practices are placing its heritage at risk, so today there is much less jungle and fewer rare species, but it is nevertheless an exotic tropical destination.

The island has always been strategically important because of its commanding position on the Malacca Strait, gateway from the Indian Ocean to the Pacific. In 1994 it was the busiest shipping lane in the world, despite the presence of modern pirates (some thought to be Indonesian military) who boarded and hijacked craft, including oil tankers.

After Portugal's Afonso de Albuquerque seized Malacca in 1511, the Sumatran sultan of Aceh converted to Islam and became increasingly powerful in the region. He was backed by the Ottoman Turks to confront the Christian aggressor, in a formula that brings to mind world politics today.

Tomé Pires was part of Albuquerque's force and wrote a detailed account of Portuguese exploits. He visited Sumatra in 1516, reporting that:

> ... most of the kings are Moors [Muslims] and some are heathens; and in the heathen country some men make a practice of eating their enemies when they capture them.[1]

He described the Aceh sultan as 'a Moor, a knightly man among his neighbours [who] uses piracy when he sees an opportunity'.[2]

On his way back to Lisbon Albuquerque overloaded his flagship *Flor de la Mar* with booty from Malacca, which had been the wealthiest sultanate in the region. The cargo reputedly included two solid gold statues of elephants, each weighing a tonne. The ship got no further than the Sumatran coast before it sank. Apparently forgetting that his duties as captain required that he should only abandon ship after all others were safe, Albuquerque had two of his sailors tie him to a raft and was saved, while all other hands perished. Professional bounty hunters consider the *Flor de la Mar* as the world's most fabulous sunken treasure ship, valued at over a billion US dollars, and in the 1980s the Suharto family formed a Singapore-backed syndicate to locate and salvage it. There are some, however, who believe the hunt is in vain because the precious cargo was salvaged at the time by the sultan of Jambi, and assert that the story is just one of the many mirages chased by the colourful international fraternity of treasure-seekers.

If the treasure was more than a mirage, some of it may well have been dislodged by the impact of the December 2004 Indian Ocean earthquake on Sumatra. Around 228,000 people are estimated to have died, most from the effects of the tsunamis that devastated coastal communities in its wake, affecting 14 countries. In Sumatra the Muslim province of Aceh was the most severely hit.

The Acehnese had fought for their independence for centuries before that time, against the Dutch and the modern state of Indonesia, with their political aspirations being represented in modern times by *Gerakin Aceh Merdeka* (GAM), the Free Aceh Movement. A ceasefire declared by GAM in the aftermath of the tsunami represented one of its few positive effects, leading as it did to talks with the Indonesian government and the signing of a peace accord on 15 August 2005, by which Indonesian troops were withdrawn and GAM disarmed. Elections followed in December 2006, in which GAM candidates won a majority, and the area was designated as a special autonomous territory.

✣ ✣ ✣ ✣ ✣

Far from being a nightmare trip, the voyage to Pekanbaru was quite beautiful, although marred by a couple of heart-stopping incidents.

There was only one other gringo on board, a male back-packer in a distant part of the boat. My immediate neighbours were two friendly young families with three small children between them. They had converted cabin 67 into a virtual penthouse by removing the demarcation slats and joining three cabins together. Opposite was a statuesque Muslim countrywoman in her 60s who sat bolt upright, darting occasional inquisitive glances in my direction and tucking regularly into a hamper of healthy peasant fare.

The first heart-stopper came when a police launch gave chase soon after departure, sirens wailing. I thought of the cursed slip of paper left at the border post and hastily repacked my baggage and donned shoes to prepare for a dignified exit in the case of arrest. A team boarded the boat, but left without searching it—they were perhaps just bringing along a forgotten package.

The initial part of the day was spent weaving between islands to glimpses of fishermen skimming past on *praus* or outrigger canoes, and of distant villages built on stilts above the water. We were on the high seas, with a considerable swell at times, but hanging one's head out of the luxury porthole into the salty wind kept nausea at bay.

As evening fell, shipboard life grew busy, with distribution of an evening meal, each passenger receiving a brown-paper package tied with string. It contained a dollop of garlicky rice, a dubious-looking boiled egg and a dob of chili sauce.

We reached the estuary of a large Limpopo-like river, after a brief stop during which lads selling lychees leapt aboard. A few passengers embarked, and we suddenly cast off again. As the lychee sellers jumped off, wads of rupiahs were tossed any old way at them, some falling short of their mark and sinking to the river bottom.

Then began a 160-km voyage up the magnificent Siak river. During it I day-dreamed about the mission ahead; the prospect of returning to the East Timorese mountains and seeing the guerrillas again provided a warm contentment. Natan had also discussed the possibility of a prison interview with Xanana Gusmão on my way through Jakarta. But it was all still thousands of kilometres away, with many barriers to cross. Sleep eventually came, but not before further scares. At one point in the river we were unexpectedly boarded by some military pug-uglies who stomped about generally and appeared to be searching the hold. I supposed this might be an arms-smuggling route for GAM, hence their nervousness.

Further along, we were stopped at a military checkpoint. I had just dozed off when the boat ground to a halt. Looking sleepily out the porthole, I stared straight into the eyes of several Indonesian officers on the bridge of a patrol-boat alongside. These were the same people I'd been writing about as human rights violators for the past 19 years and, indeed, some of them may even have served in Timor. My greatest dread was of falling into the hands of the military: I could handle being caught as an illegal and being turned back or expelled by the immigration department or the police, but I hoped against hope to avoid that fate. During 16 years in Lisbon I had interviewed probably hundreds of East Timorese ex-prisoners, and the military's Gestapo-like behaviour had become sickeningly familiar. I was gradually getting used to these encounters however, and my nerves were steadier.

A full moon rose over the river. The water was still and flat, bordered with rushes; small fishing craft passed occasionally. It later turned a rusty blood-red, maybe with oil from the Caltex derricks, the first flames of which could be seen through the jungle. As dawn approached, soft sheets of lightning lit the sky, followed by heavy rain.

As we neared Pekanbaru the rain turned to a steady drizzle and the vegetation changed from marshy mangrove to pure tropical rainforest with all its rich variations of green. The colour of the water was not due to the oil, it seemed, but to an infestation of red algae.

The ferry docked late in the afternoon. I had decided to travel on by road as rapidly as possible, hoping to reach the hill town of Bukittinggi, where there was a military museum with some exhibits highlighting campaigns in East Timor. I had made a last-minute bid in Hong Kong to interest ITN in the journey and persuade them to send a camera operator with me (bending Natan's confidentiality rules). They had refused. 'You say you're banned, but you're going to travel through Indonesia, interview a guerrilla commander in the Timor mountains, and interview Xanana as well!' the bureau chief laughed scornfully. That possibility having been shafted, I intended to at least scout locations for a documentary that I might film on a return trip, and the Bukittinggi museum sounded promising.

Pekanbaru bus station was a seething mass of petty crooks and hucksters who tugged at clothing and fought for luggage, offering tickets to fanciful destinations at fanciful prices.

I had decided not to learn any Indonesian beyond courtesy phrases, as a form of self-protection—the less communication, the less chance of betraying myself with inconsistent lies, or accidentally incriminating others in the case of arrest. I finally found the man who sold the real tickets to Bukittinggi, costing 6,500 rupiahs. He stood in front of a reasonable-looking bus. After buying the ticket I asked him optimistically if it had air-conditioning. 'It isn't *this* bus!' he explained, pointing to a rusting wreck nearby, which departed at 6 pm. Its air-conditioning consisted of the door being tied permanently open with a piece of string.

I was given seat number 1, which had lost the original virtues of its design when a box was fixed underneath it to reduce the distance from legs to floor, so that the only possible sitting position was perched on the exact tip of one's coccyx, with arse-numbing consequences. I had managed to have a rapid full-body wash at a tap in a hotel laundry, but had been unable to change my evil-smelling clothes, and was conscious that I stank. Chain-smoking *kreteks* seemed to be a sensible antidote. I doubted it was appropriate behaviour for a woman in an Islamic setting, but I was by now feeling the effects of nervous exhaustion, so took the risk.

My Sumatran travelling companions, who turned out to be charming, looked merely amused. My neighbour over the aisle was a well-dressed, elderly woman from Bukittinggi who was travelling with her adult daughter, a granddaughter about 12, and an adolescent boy. The women's clothes were all of silks and fine printed cottons. Behind me was a man in his 60s, of educated, middle-class appearance, who wore a *pitji*, the soft black cap that had been a symbol of nationalism in the Sukarno era. Like all of them, he indicated with smiles and gestures where to put my luggage, and where the next stop was. They were protective of the poor foreigner without a word of their language.

I had understood from the guidebook that the journey was four hours, but was horrified to discover that I had misread it and faced 12 hours in the hell-seat, with arrival at Bukittinggi set for dawn next day.

However, there was a reprieve that allowed a private insight into the gentle society of my fellow travellers. Four hours along the road we stopped at a sort of travellers' aid station with restaurant.

The women went to a large circular platform covered with the ubiquitous linoleum, in a room at the back. Opposite was a kitchen with a huge open fire with water on the boil and food in preparation. Behind it was a latrine area.

Shoes were removed before climbing on to the platform, which had long bolsters around the edge, serving as pillows.

The women then arranged themselves with a natural symmetry into a starfish pattern, feet at the centre, like synchronised swimmers in a 1950s Esther Williams movie. Most had crisp cotton cloths to lay over them. We slept for about three hours, then it was prayer time for some.

My elderly neighbour and a couple of other women lay down their prayer mats facing Mecca and donned white embroidered headdresses. At times they sat in meditation, either motionless or mouthing prayers soundlessly; at other times they stood and prayed. Sometimes they seemed to break off to gossip to each other, as though they were discussing the price of eggs.

The lavatories were of the Asian hole-in-the-ground variety, behind a concrete screen. They and the bathing facilities were scrupulously clean, thanks to the custom of separating clean and contaminated water, never putting soap in the main tank or attempting to wash in it, but using it as a source to sluice the toilet and to wash the body.

Here the outward modesty of these Islamic women gave way to a complete familiarity and casualness about bodies. They stripped off outer layers of clothes, and squatted to wash their genitals as they chatted to each other, all without a trace of inhibition. During feminist debates of the 1970s between Third World and Western women, the former had argued that the imprisoning dress codes Islamic women accepted gave them a remarkable inner freedom. I'm not sure about this argument, but could imagine how these women might gossip together about their macho, polygamous men in this free world-within-a-world, and the fun and vitriolic jokes that might pass in comparing sexual notes.

The rest-stop concluded with a hearty meal washed down with the gritty, aromatic coffee of Indonesia, and the journey continued. We entered Bukittinggi as the sun was rising.

I decided to treat myself to a regular hotel instead of a *losmen*. Here began a problem that was to plague the journey.

The reception clerk gave me a form to fill in and demanded my passport, which was compulsory to register when checking into the hotel. (They hadn't asked for it in Tanjung Pinang, but that was probably because it had been too humble an establishment to count.) It was a system of social control I knew well from Portugal, where it had been adopted in the years of the Salazar dictatorship and remained in force after the 1974 revolution, a relic of the past. The registration slips would be collected at the end of each day and would eventually end up at the police station.

I quickly suggested taking the form to my room to complete, indicating my exhausted state and unwieldy luggage, with the passport somewhere at the bottom. Thinking through the problem, I decided it would be crazy to write in a false name, but would instead write in my first two Christian names, or part thereof, and leave off the surname. 'Jill Rosemary JOLLIFFE' therefore became 'Jill ROSE'. If they checked against the passport and challenged it, I'd just say I'd forgotten to write it in full—a weak excuse, but not falsification. In future I would always attempt to fill out the form myself and avoid showing the passport. The principle was fine, except that I automatically signed my full signature. In nervous dismay I then tried to alter it, creating an appalling smudged mess. I was a truly hopeless undercover agent, more like Groucho Marx. I would have to hope for the best, and book out as early as possible in the morning. Mercifully, there were no repercussions. But then Bukittinggi had been the centre of an anti-Javanese military revolt in 1955, so maybe they weren't all that worried about pleasing the regime.

There was a strong sense of history about the town, set at 930 metres above sea level. With its ornate pony traps, fort, and antique clock-tower, it had the feel of a hill-station from the British Raj.

The exhibits in the military museum interested me a lot. There were two showcases containing captured weapons and uniforms of East Timorese guerrillas, from a military operation in the late 1970s. There was also the flag of the Indonesian unit involved, a balance sheet of the operation, a list of those who participated, and a captured FRETILIN flag. It had photos and the ID card of a FRETILIN leader called Araújo, who had been killed.

The second of the two showcases featured photos of Operation Fence-of-Legs, the 1981 military operation in which young Timorese had been forced to act as human shields in a territory-wide hunt for guerrillas. Some of these had been published abroad and did not present anything new in the way of documentation—only the setting in which they were presented gave them some morbid curiosity value.

There was something sad about the pictures of Araújo, whose death was being commemorated in this Indonesian provincial museum as an illustration of the army's successes in the former Portuguese colony, with his Timorese family almost certainly unaware these documents existed or even of the exact details of his death.

I decided the museum could be useful for a future documentary, and left on another bone-shaker of a bus for a 40-hour journey direct to Jakarta, crossing on a ferry between Sumatra and Java islands.

I had decided to book into the Borneo Hostel in Jalan Jaksa, the busy downtown neighbourhood of Jakarta favoured by Australian backpackers, where it should be easier to fade into the tourist scenery, and from where the Timorese could be contacted.

I arrived filthy and exhausted on 9 July. The passport routine went off without a hitch this time, but I then set fire to my second hotel room. On entry, it was swarming with potentially malarial mosquitos, so I lit a repellent coil, tossed off my clothes and headed for the refreshing cold water of the *mandi*. There was a trendy backpackers' bar adjoining the room, from which came the sound of laughter and clinking glasses. It suddenly gave way to coughing, shouting and the smell of acrid fumes. A leap into the bedroom revealed a mound of burning clothes, which I had tossed over the mosquito coil. Clouds of smoke were billowing out the window onto the bar—and, worse, under the door, which faced into the reception area. The blaze was effectively subdued with a frantic application of dippers of water. Amazingly, no-one seemed to notice on a lasting basis, but I wondered if my subconscious was issuing a warning to desist from this perilous adventure.

3

The Long Wait

Jakarta, 9–20 July 1994

With a population of almost 17 million, Jakarta is the tenth-largest city in the world. It is six degrees south of the equator but is also set on a plain, so that in the hottest period of the year temperatures are regularly around 35 °C and it is an effort to perform everyday tasks. The body is rapidly debilitated and the humidity, noise, dust and unceasing movement of traffic invades the brain. Malaria is endemic. The middle class flee the capital for the cool hills of Bandung at this time.

Soldiers swagger around the central Merdeka Square flanked by Suharto's palace. They cruise in vehicles with smoked-glass windows or ply to and fro on the back of troop-carriers. Billboards with gigantic images of the president are their backdrop, so that they are like figures moving on a stage set. In one the president appears to be The Great Harvester, wearing a conical peasant hat and holding blades of rice in his hand. In another he is The Great Engineer, inspecting a factory as the wheels of industry turn behind him. The extras in the performance are the common people who manoeuvre their food carts or wagons through the massive waves of traffic. On the inner-city ring roads, six lanes of speeding cars bear down on the pedestrian. It is near-impossible to cross, and traffic lights are about half a kilometre apart but, with experience, one masters techniques to cross and survive, all requiring a strong nerve.

My first task in the city was to find the East Timorese, who kept a low profile. I telephoned the number Natan had given, at regular intervals. *'Tidak'*, indicating 'not here', was all I understood from the Indonesian phrases that came back, raising doubt about whether it was the right number. Portuguese was the language of the resistance, but there were no Portuguese speakers there, although they seemed to understand a little English. Finally, there was a message in slow English: 'F.F. said to go to the meeting place tomorrow, 4 pm.' *F.F.?* Pronounced *effie effie*, in the Portuguese manner, it was an introduction to the person who would plan and accompany my adventures of the next weeks and become a friend in the process.

The next day, a Sunday, I trekked to the Monas monument clinging to the Berlitz travel guide to Thailand. It was a favourite weekend leisure spot and was buzzing with people. Hawkers laid out cheap toys, novelties and clothing in a giant patchwork at the base of the monument, with delicious aromas wafting from the carts of noodle sellers.

I stationed myself near the entrance and waited, a foolish white woman standing out in the crowd, peering intently at passing faces to distinguish between Indonesian and Timorese features. A man stopped and lingered. He seemed to be signalling with his eyes, gesturing to follow. But was he Timorese? Perhaps he was INTEL, the secret police. I moved to follow, then hesitated. After several such false starts, what should have been obvious from the beginning become evident: if a woman stands on a street corner alone, men will always approach her to accompany them. The great master spy had been mistaken for a prostitute and almost walked away tamely with the first man who beckoned.

After several hours of waiting it was clear F.F. was not going to show.

The meeting was re-scheduled by phone for the same time the next day. After a passing parade similar to that of the previous day, a man of medium height with longish hair and a large floppy hat stopped and suggested I follow him.

This case looked more authentic, but caution was required. 'Do you speak Portuguese?', I asked in that language. *'Falo, falo'*, ('I speak it, I speak it') he replied. It was F.F.

Then began the first of a series of regular meetings to plan the journey to meet Konis Santana. We found an isolated place in the park where we sat and talked, while three youths who had meanwhile appeared kept watch some distance away. Talking was important to operatives of the Timorese underground in Jakarta. They needed information about events in the outside world. The Indonesian newspapers were still heavily censored, and although they could tune in to the BBC for independent news sources, they lived in a hot-house atmosphere in which objective political assessments were at a premium. They needed to bounce ideas off others, to hear of the many international variables at work for and against their movement for self-determination, and to receive news of Timorese working abroad.

Here I had my first glimpse of the other members of F.F.'s resistance circle. During conversation I sneaked curious glances at their faces to size them up, as far as I could without seeming impolite. They smiled shyly and were delighted with my arrival.

Tommy was F.F.'s right-hand man. He was small and thin with a bony face. Although he treated his allocated resistance tasks with deadly seriousness he was a cheery character, dreaming up jokes and humming the latest songs from the Indonesian Top 10. He was excellent for keeping spirits high. He had a joke about *bakso*, the favourite 20c fishball dinner we often bought from the evening noodle seller when we were travelling together. 'Why are *bakso* balls round?' he would ask, then pause for the inevitable shrug of defeat. 'Because this is how they make them!' came the triumphant reply, as he mimicked the cook rolling them in his armpits.

I warmed to Rui, who became a regular employee of the UN High Commission for Refugees in Dili after liberation.

By contrast with Tommy he was earnest in demeanour and pondered every statement as he searched for an answer. He had a wide, gentle face with an illuminating smile and it came as no surprise when I learnt later that he had studied for the priesthood.

The third member of the crew in those first days was Zely, who was considerably younger than the others and seemed to be an agent-in-training. He could have been 16 or 17. There were many people that young playing key roles—rather worrying, considering the danger of it. It went almost without saying that if they were arrested they would be tortured. Timorese resistance supporters were an endangered species in the sprawling, polluted metropolis of Jakarta in 1994.

'We need you to write a letter to Konis Santana explaining your aims,' F.F. explained, 'and another to Xanana Gusmão with the interview questions you'd like to put to him. We'll send a courier to East Timor immediately, and then must wait for his return with Santana's answer.'

In the next days they taught me the rules of surviving in the city without detection. There were endless security measures to be observed. There were two sorts of taxis in Jakarta, regular air-conditioned sedan cars, and the three-wheeled *bejak* vehicles, the preferred transport of the poor, which were noisy and open to the exhaust fumes blanketing the traffic lanes.

We never spoke to each other in the regular taxis. Members of Kopassus, the feared special forces battalion, took regular turns at driving these taxis to collect intelligence, with tape recorders tucked under the seats. Whether they were from Kopassus or other intelligence agencies, it was not difficult to spot the secret police, who wore a de facto uniform: cropped hair, trim moustache, Rolex watch and Ray-Ban sunglasses. With time, one could sense their presence instinctively. The Timorese were so alert to these potential enemies that their eye would automatically move to one of them in a crowd.

'Never take one taxi straight to a destination,' F.F. instructed, 'change several times to ensure you're not followed. And remember that the *bejak* drivers are the most trustworthy. They're just poor people, as oppressed as we are.'

There were a series of further meetings in the next days, at which I delivered the letters and a tape-recorded message for Gusmão with an outline of interview questions, and learnt more about conditions in Jakarta and the East Timor mountains. Meetings were usually set for soon after sunset in the Monas park area, and could sometimes be hair-raising. Like any park in the centre of a big metropolis, strange people came out to play after dark. There were lovers of all inclinations trysting and a few normal people just strolling, but there were also prostitutes, drug dealers, muggers and the ubiquitous secret police watching it all.

My diary of 14 July 1994 noted: 'The toll of the waiting game on nerves is heightened by the way I meet my companions—in parks after dark, the equivalent of New York's Central Park. Sometimes I have more fear of being robbed and beaten up than being detected by authorities.'

Our meetings usually went off without a hitch, but one night we had agreed to meet at a particularly dark and remote corner of Monas. I had checked carefully to see I wasn't being followed. Coming close to the meeting point, where the shadowy forms of a few non-Timorese were also circulating, a man swung in behind me. He was a few metres away, but as I moved towards them, he was closing the distance between us, almost certainly to accost or attack me, the sole white person in this dubious park after dark without an apparent reason. It was necessary to reach F.F. quickly, but then it occurred that the man could be an INTEL agent. Recognising the Timorese under these circumstances could mean their arrest. They came into view but I kept walking. Fortunately, Tommy saw the dilemma and took a decision. Just as the man was right on my heels, within touching distance, he stepped forward and said to me cheerfully: 'Hi, glad you could come, how are you?' The pursuer blended rapidly into the night.

Most days didn't offer so much drama, and I settled in for the long wait for Santana's reply, killing time by pounding the pavements of this vast tropical city for hours and days on end.

I walked, observing people and buildings, sampling the local food and losing myself in suburban markets that sprawled over several hectares. I was walking off nervous energy at the same time as I was discovering new worlds.

Under the Monas monument where I had first waited for F.F., I found there were a series of dioramas describing scenes from Indonesian history. Entry was free, so the display served as a poor people's movie-house, and for indoctrination. There were always families moving in clumps past each instructive scene, which included depictions of the alleged coup orchestrated by Communists in 1965, with the bodies of generals being pulled from wells, and scenes from the story of the heroic Indonesian army's fight to free the people of both Irian Jaya and East Timor. The general area where the public milled around was dim and gave greater emphasis to the illuminated plasticine-like figures, except that in some cases light globes had given out and not been replaced, so people had to peer keenly into the glass cases, faces close, trying to make sense of what they saw. But perhaps even when they saw the figures they didn't make sense.

The *Lonely Planet* guide described exhibits in the army museum concerning East Timor campaigns. It had long been rumoured that the personal weapon of Nicolau Lobato, first commander of the guerrilla resistance, was displayed, having been taken from him at the time of his death, and

I really wanted to see it. F.F. and my other minders advised against it, saying that the army attendants there took a special interest in visitors and I risked my identity being exposed. I decided to go anyway.

At the entrance there was a tank with a sign saying it had been used in Operation Seroja, the December 1975 air, sea and land attack on East Timor. Inside, the attendants were uniformed army officers who took a close interest in guests, just as F.F. had said. There was a visitors' book that was obligatory to sign, so I wrote an unhurried 'Jill Rose' and then began to move around the exhibits, trying not to register expression or linger too long in front of those where East Timor figured.

The story of Nicolau's gun had been exaggerated. A semi-automatic G-3 rifle said to have been captured in Timor was there, just as there had been one in Bukittinggi, but nothing to indicate it had belonged to Nicolau, and certainly no triumphalist display concerning him.

It probably had been taken from him, and the absence of a label merely expressed the Indonesian military's policy of obliterating all traces of his life. He had been surrounded and killed in an Indonesian operation in the central mountains on the last day of 1978 and his body brought down to Dili. Indonesian and Timorese officials were photographed with the bullet-ridden corpse of this handsome hero at the airport, but then it disappeared. No-one knows where Nicolau was buried, or if indeed he was buried. There was a rumour that President Suharto had telephoned General Dading Kalbuadi, the East Timor commander, and ordered him to send him Lobato's head and that subsequently it had been hacked off, paraded around some districts of East Timor and then dispatched to him in Jakarta. There was, therefore, considerable excitement in 2004 when a headless skeleton was found buried deep in the garden of Dading Kalbuadi's former Dili residence, by then home to FRETILIN

Prime Minister Mari Alkatiri. The remains were sent for forensic testing in a Darwin laboratory, but no results had been announced by early 2010.

Nicolau and his family had never been far from my thoughts in the 19 years since the invasion. He was a man with a magnetic presence: reserved, good-looking and quintessentially East Timorese. In 1975 he and his wife Isabel came frequently to the Hotel Turismo where I stayed, with their toddler son José, known as 'Zezinho'. I used to admire them from a distance. She was as beautiful as he was handsome, and the baby had inherited the best of both of them; they seemed to be the model Timorese nationalist family. I talked to them occasionally and learnt that, after a period in a Jesuit seminary, Nicolau had joined the Portuguese civil service, while studying economics at night. Unlike his better-known nationalist counterparts, he had not gone to Lisbon to study, and was far from being a Marxist fire-brand. He became prime minister in FRETILIN's first government, lasting ten days, and then took to the mountains to lead the guerrillas. Later I taught English to Isabel (having caved in to popular demand to give lessons to a group of people each morning before I began work as a journalist).

They had suffered a cruel fate. When the Indonesian army landed in Dili on 7 December 1975, Isabel was one of many East Timorese and Chinese publicly executed on Dili wharf, having been pointed out by a collaborator. She managed to thrust two-year-old Zezinho into the arms of her sister before she was dragged to her death. In his autobiography Xanana Gusmão described coming across Nicolau near their mountain encampment soon before his death. He was weighed down by the enormous responsibility of leading the guerrilla resistance and was weeping helplessly for his dead wife and lost child.

What I did find in the army museum was a diorama dedicated to the 'liberation' of East Timor. On the left it showed a group of people welcoming Indonesian troops, who must have been modelled from photos because they bore a close resemblance to real people—Arnaldo de Araújo, the Indonesian-installed governor, Francisco Lopes da Cruz, a leader of the pro-Indonesian movement, and Mario Carrascalão, who was to become governor in a later period. To the right was a scene with a dying guerrilla, perhaps Nicolau, surrounded by Indonesian soldiers.

The days were dragging on and still there was no conclusive word from the East Timor mountains. One courier had returned to Dili from delivering a letter to Comandante Mate Resto, and my diary recorded that the reply was not altogether satisfactory. '[They are] in agreement that I should go,' I wrote, 'but they want me to go via the capital, which I am resisting as unsafe.' It was feared that a second courier, thought to be bringing a reply from Nino Konis Santana, may have been caught up in rioting and its aftermath in Dili, so hadn't contacted base.

During the continued wait I discussed with F.F. and Tommy the possibility of setting up two meetings in Jakarta, which needed careful preparation.

I wanted to meet Pascal Mallet, the Agence France-Presse correspondent who was to have accompanied the press group travelling with the 1991 Portuguese parliamentary delegation. We had corresponded at the time, and the idea was driven by curiosity to know him, but also out of the lingering hope that it still might be possible to find a freelance photographer or television camera operator to also travel to the mountains.

The other person I wanted to see was Hadj Princen, a.k.a. 'Poncke', a Dutch civil rights activist of Indonesian nationality who had worked doggedly in support of the East Timorese. He had given practical and psychological support to the many young people serving long-term prison sentences in Jakarta and elsewhere since the early 1980s.

I had met him in Lisbon a few years before and valued his judgement on the Indonesian political situation. We both understood those years were a prelude to the inevitable fall of Suharto. How was it going to pan out? Who would be the players? Were there dissidents in the armed forces? These were the questions we had tossed around in Portugal and it would be useful to continue our discussion.

It would not be easy to organise the meetings with watertight security, but F.F. set about the task. The problem with contacting Pascal Mallet was that Agence France-Presse shared a building with the Australian Broadcasting Corporation in Jakarta. Australia was still Indonesia's staunch ally on the East Timor question and the ABC's reporting was conciliatory. Its uncritical broadcasts led Indonesian democrats to tune out and connect to the BBC for independent information. Moreover, because of my writing and the ban by Jakarta I was notorious among Australian diplomats, and the journalists mixed regularly with them. I did not trust the embassy, and feared that if my presence in Indonesia was known there, word could soon reach the security police.

Tommy had a plan that worked like a charm. We went to the France-Presse office in the evening, after he had called the journalist to say he wanted to see him. I waited outside in the dark while he went in to convince him to come and meet an unnamed person, which he did without demurring. He appeared pleasantly surprised when I introduced myself, and invited both of us to a restaurant to talk.

He and Tommy got on well and chatted a lot in Indonesian about East Timor. Then Pascal turned to me, referring to the Indonesian foreign minister's recent heart attack: 'So you're really going to the East Timor jungles? Ali Alatas will have a second seizure if he finds out!'

Princen was a legend in Indonesia. He had been raised in Holland by freethinking parents and been attracted to anarchist ideas. After Holland was occupied by the Nazis, he made his way out of the country in a bid to reach England and enlist, but instead was captured and put in a concentration camp.

He later joined the Dutch army and was sent to fight in the so-called police action to restore colonial rule against Indonesian nationalists. In 1948 he deserted, to fight with them against his compatriots. Sukarno, Indonesia's founding president, decorated him with the Guerrilla Star, Indonesia's highest honour. He took out Indonesian citizenship, converted to Islam, and was elected to parliament in 1956. In Holland he was branded a traitor and banned from returning to his homeland until the closing years of his life.

Unlike many opponents of the Suharto regime who had never criticised the populist Sukarno, his record on political freedom was thoroughgoing. He was imprisoned by both Sukarno and Suharto for his defence of human rights, serving a total of eight-and-a-half years in prison.

In the early 1970s Princen founded the Indonesian Legal Aid Institute (YLBHI). Despite his critical role, his prestige in Indonesia always remained high because of his role in the independence struggle. But he stood out from other political critics because of his early stand in support of East Timorese self-determination, a cause which was taboo even in the most progressive circles, where nationalism reigned supreme.

In later years he suffered mutilating surgery for skin cancer and then a series of near-fatal strokes. Yet his luminous spirit shone through his crippled wreck of a body, and he continued his work as before.

Extensive precautions were taken for our meeting, with members of F.F.'s group being mobilised as look-outs. We met at a food stall in the deserted Anco theme park outside the capital, a Jakartan version of Melbourne's Luna Park, and resumed the discussion we had left off in Lisbon.

His input was important for an accurate evaluation of the internal situation in Indonesia. I needed this intelligence on several counts: as a journalist, for my safe travel, and to give a considered assessment to the Timorese guerrilla leadership if they asked me, seeing they were cut off from regular communication with the wider world.

It was the last time I saw Princen, who was to die in 2002. We spoke several more times on the phone, and he did everything to support my journey to visit Santana. I used his bank account to receive money from my account in Portugal without my name appearing, and he helped in a thousand other small ways with advice and practical measures. I was privileged to know this rare free spirit.

There were signs that we might be leaving, none too soon for me. I had been in Jakarta for less than a fortnight, but it had seemed like an eternity.

I continued to wander the streets. Jakarta bookshops offered slim pickings, but occasionally I found a treasure. I was looking for a book to accompany me on the journey ahead. I found it in an Oxford University Press paperback, *Unbeaten Tracks in Islands of the Far East: Experiences of a Naturalist's Wife in the 1880s*, by Anna Forbes.[3] Some years before I had paid £135 for a copy of Henry Forbes's *A Naturalist's Wanderings in the Eastern Archipelago*, a second edition acquired from Blackwell's Bookshop in Oxford. I had first read it when researching a book 20 years before. He had followed in the footsteps of Darwin's colleague Alfred Russel Wallace, who had gone to East Timor in the 1860s, but the Forbes account was more detailed and rich, and his observations on Timorese customs are still useful to the contemporary traveller. He had ridden through all the traditional kingdoms without ever seeing a Portuguese, effectively knocking on the door at each border for admission from the local ruler, demonstrating that tribal society was still intact 300 years or so after the Portuguese had arrived.

By the late 19th century they had not penetrated their supposed colony, but remained perched on the coast, living out the fantasy of conquest.

At the end of Forbes's detailed scientific description is the dramatic account of his hastened return to Dili on receiving news that his wife Anna (in truth his new bride—they were on their honeymoon!) was at death's door, having been stricken with malaria. The pair were unconventional travellers and had arrived in Dili after a long and lively journey along the Indonesian archipelago by sea; my route was roughly similar to theirs. The Portuguese governor Bento da França had invited them to stay in his palace, which they declined. They scandalised polite society by instead building a traditional house near the Timorese hamlet of Fatunaba, in the hills behind Dili. It was here that Henry left Anna while he conducted his expedition into the mountains, an arrangement that they both considered natural and sensible. He did not realise that the Timorese woman entrusted with her care was half-mad and would turn on her, first stealing her belongings, then abandoning her when the fever took hold. She fought for survival in the next weeks, delirious and fending off the rats trying to steal her last food, until by an enormous effort of will she finally obtained help.

Mrs Forbes was a woman after my own heart, and now I had found a version of her story in her own words, based on diaries. She would be my companion on the quest for Santana.

On 20 July I recorded in my diary:

> Yes, we're off! Leaving tomorrow for Lombok, with escort of two. Frantic shopping for equipment and supplies, last-minute treats (like American breakfast, pancakes and maple syrup, in 5-star hotel) to compensate for rough travel ahead.

4
Cat and Mouse with INTEL

Denpasar to Ende, 21–29 July 1994

The three of us were in high spirits as we boarded a long-haul bus bound for Bali, from where we would change for Lombok, bringing us half-way to Timor. The trip to Denpasar, the Balinese capital, would take 30 hours, and I was accompanied by Tommy and F.F. It was a chance to have some of the in-depth discussions we didn't have time for under the pressured circumstances of our meetings at Monas. The Timorese underground in Jakarta was starved for information about the wider world, which they needed to determine their strategy, and they were full of questions. I didn't want to be in the position of offering political advice and stressed that a journalist needs to keep a distance from political parties and factions to maintain a critical spirit. Any political assessments I offered were therefore purely personal opinions and they should always seek counterbalancing views. They respected that, and we ranged over myriad topics: how their refugees lived in Portugal, whether information they were sending out was having any effect, whether the Australian government, or the US, might change its stand of supporting the Suharto dictatorship, and so on.

I also learnt about F.F.'s underground network. It was unique among Timorese resistance groups active in Indonesia and East Timor in declaring itself to be socialist. The *Associação Socialista de Timor* (Timorese Socialist Association—AST) had been formed a few years before as a split-off from the FRETILIN party. Its main stated aims were to support the guerrilla struggle, and Timorese students, workers and political prisoners in Indonesia. Its leaders encouraged those living there not to boycott political life but to become active in unions, university politics and the human rights struggle of their Indonesian brothers and sisters at the same time as they presented their case for East Timor's independence. This was difficult, because even Indonesia's most radical activists argued that 'Tim-Tim' belonged to them. Some of the other Timorese groups considered AST extremist and criticised its break with the mainstream FRETILIN, and both sides carried a lot of political baggage from past political differences. Nevertheless they had won respect by their hands-on performance. F.F. had a good relationship with Xanana Gusmão and communicated regularly with him in Cipinang prison via the underground mail service, as well as with those fighting in the mountains. I was amazed to see that his group had succeeded in publishing nationalist tracts in Portuguese at an Indonesian printer in Jakarta, a highly dangerous activity. They were impressive to read, because they showed the Timorese sounding out ideas, analysing tentatively, finding their way—in short, thinking and debating, of which there had been too little in the development of their movement in my opinion. The texts looked peculiar because the courageous Indonesian printer did not have Portuguese accents, which are essential to pronunciation, so a new language had been born: Portuguese-as-written-by-clandestine-printer-in-Indonesia.

F.F. was fluent in Portuguese as well as in English, and it was our preferred language of communication. With Tommy I spoke English, although he did have some Portuguese. F.F. and I found a seat together at the back of the bus, where we conversed softly, while Tommy sat separately towards the front, as a security precaution. I was the only foreigner on the bus, and we had to take care not to be heard talking

Portuguese, which was considered by the secret police as a language of the resistance.

Soon we were speeding through the countryside, popular Indonesian music blaring through the loudspeakers as the kilometres disappeared behind us, whizzing past bamboo hamlets, bullock carts and a variety of small motorised vehicles. We were travelling eastward along the north coast of the great island of Java, from Jakarta to Cirebon to Semarang, Surabaya and hence to its eastern tip, where the bus would board the ferry to Bali, 1,193 km from the Indonesian capital.

The tickets for the three of us had cost around US$300, a substantial slice of my meagre budget, but any long bus journey in Indonesia includes all meals, with scheduled stops at restaurants. There were also toilet stops that gave time for a decent coffee. In Indonesia it is unnecessary to carry toiletries because small towels of the variety that have 'Good Morning!' written in Chinese and English are available at every restaurant, with miniature packs of soap, toothpaste and brushes. The savvy traveller thus advances unfettered by luggage.

When we met to catch the bus F.F. had given me the slightly alarming news that Liem Soei Long, a London-based Indonesian activist working for Tapol, the political prisoners' organisation, had been arrested soon after arriving in the country on the Singapore ferry by the same route I had used. He had been interrogated for two days. We instinctively increased our vigilance.

Somewhere along the road three men of military demeanour, but in plain clothes, boarded the bus—cropped hair, neat moustaches, two in their 40s, the other a little older. They began to take an interest in us. First they engaged Tommy in conversation, asking who we were and where we were going. 'We can never hide, they know who we are,' observed F.F., pointing to his curly hair, which makes the

Timorese distinctive in Indonesia. Tommy answered with great care. They knew he was with us, because we always sat together at the coffee stops, and they could see that there were two Timorese with a foreigner. The next time we stopped, Tommy whispered that he had found out they were all on their way back to East Timor to report for duty. Moreover, the older one was a military judge—a hanging judge, no doubt, I thought. As we headed for Surabaya, we realised the situation was untenable. At the last stop they had approached me in a friendly way with their questions. I had already prepared a story, the 'Sydney real estate agent' routine, embellished by a chance meeting with two nice lads who were accompanying me to Bali where I wanted to buy some weavings, and needed their advice on the best traditional cloths. I told them we were going to Bali, no further, and then returning to Jakarta. They backed off, but we knew that to continue would spell trouble. We would be forfeiting our tickets half-way through the journey, but there was no alternative. When the bus stopped at Surabaya and passengers were entering the café, we grabbed our luggage and fled. We held a quick conference, deciding that F.F. would return to Jakarta to re-organise the expedition, while I would travel on in the direction of Timor after pausing to allow the sinister trio to get ahead of me. Tommy would continue to accompany me, but always in the bus behind, never in the same.

I wasn't in the mood to reflect too much about Surabaya, which was a busy industrial port with a distinguished history in Indonesia's independence battle—Bertolt Brecht had paid tribute to it in his creation of the character Surabaya Johnny, but I had noticed that Mrs Forbes had come across a mummified mermaid and merman in Surabaya, which tended to wash away the bad taste our brush with the INTEL agents had given. She and Henry had sailed from Batavia (as Jakarta was known then) via Semarang, with the plan of catching a different boat to Macassar, on present-day Sulawesi.

There was a five-day wait, so they explored the town, which she described as 'of no mean size, and … a busy seat of trade'. She recorded entering a Chinese shop to make some purchases, and seeing 'a wonderful collection of curiosities':

> Among them were some carved statues of great value and interest, but most curious to us were a mummified merman and mermaid. These I had always thought to be fabulous creations of simple-minded seafarers, but those we saw were certainly sufficient to give origin to the tales we had heard of them. The upper part of the body is quite human in form, and is smooth-skinned; the face is ape-like, but human enough to suggest the comparison, only there is no hair on the head. The fore-limbs are arms with five fingers. The lower part of the body is that of a fish with scales and fins.[4]

In the same shop, she saw a newly-arrived cargo of '2000 skins of the orange-feathered bird of paradise, 800 of the king-bird, and a various lot of others', and expressed disgust at the wanton slaughter, adding 'soon we shall have lost off the face of the globe these unique and most gorgeous of the feathered tribes'. She wrote that Wallace had drawn the bird of paradise in his *Malay Archipelago* but the illustration gave 'no idea of its velvety plumage'.

On 23 July I noted in my diary that I seemed to have woken up in a Hindu temple. Arriving in the Balinese capital, I had asked a taxi driver to direct me to a cheap *losmen* but he had instead taken me to the Hotel Denpasar, which cost US$22 a night, expensive by my standards. It was certainly not a Western-style hotel, however, and provided food for thought as well as the belly. It had a series of functional rooms lining corridors in a building with various courtyards

and rooms with exotic sculpted figures—a daemonic elephant devouring a dragon, erotic naked women, an elaborate gold-leaf door with gods, evil spirits and animals depicted, alongside signs saying things like 'the blouse should fit the cloth' and 'honour the rule and the journey will be accomplished'. I wondered if that maxim could bring luck to my journey.

Sadly, I could not stay on because I had been given no choice but to present my passport and register with my real name. I decided to sleep for four hours, give the proprietor an excuse for checking out, and catch a bus to Lombok. Erase the trail.

'Sorry, but I'm leaving. I rang home and found I have friends staying at Kuta Beach,' I told him as I waved the key gaily, 'They're renting a house and want me to go and stay with them, so I'm off. Lots of parties! Thanks for everything.'

Twenty-four hours later I was installed in a non-passport-showing *losmen* in Mataram, provincial capital of the island of Lombok. I initially felt safe, as well as pleased that I was drawing closer to my destination, but began to suffer from attacks of spiralling anxiety, and recorded 'a moment of black depression, imagining the prospect of defeat'.

Reaching Lombok seemed like a moral victory because I had passed the Wallace Line, described by Alfred Russel Wallace as the dividing line between the Asian and Australian animal kingdoms. The island peoples of the Lesser Sunda group, everything east of Bali to Timor, show Polynesian and Melanesian influences and are often antagonistic to rule from Java. To them, the pale-faced Javanese are as the Han Chinese to the Tibetans.

In Mataram I fell in with a group of backpackers who were travelling to Komodo Island, sole habitat of the komodo dragon, which lay between Sumbawa, the next island in the chain, and Flores. There was no sign of the hanging judge and his friends, but I stayed an extra day to be sure, and then travelled on with them; they provided protective colouration. There was an American school teacher among them who asked an annoying lot of questions, which gave me difficulty keeping the Jane Carlton story straight. Lying in these circumstances needs to be terribly consistent and I didn't always do it. I made Jane a literary dabbler, which is how she came to know such a suspicious lot about Indonesian history and politics.

At each stop I had been telephoning back to Zely to let F.F. know where I was. We had spoken a couple of times, and agreed that the three of us would reunite in Kupang. Having a private conversation from a public telephone is a difficult business in a dictatorship. Telephone surveillance was standard practice in Indonesia and public phones were usually concentrated outside post offices, under windows where the caller was always in view of the uniformed public servants, whose role verged on the paramilitary. It was difficult to make a call without being observed and, once observed, the call could then be monitored from within the building. There were no cabins, or even partitions to give privacy from callers alongside. I finally understood the virtues of good old-fashioned red English telephone boxes. Years later, I was disappointed to see that, when East Timor became independent, the Timor Telecom public phone system they installed mimicked the Indonesian dictatorship model. Occasionally during the trip I found little gems of public phones that were just out of view of the thought police—perhaps the architect for those particular post offices had been a freethinker.

The ferry from Sumbawa to Komodo Island and Flores left from Bima, on the eastern tip of the island. I bought my ticket early in my anxiety to move on. There was an hour or so to wait, so I was relieved when the crew finally lowered the gang-plank to receive the passengers. I picked up my luggage to board but as I did glanced around and saw the three characters from the Bali bus heading towards the boat. They saw me at the same time. It was obvious I had not stopped at Bali and, no doubt, there had been much comment when we left the bus. Trapped, I pondered my choices. To cut and run was not the answer. Better to remain calm and act normally—and hope to hell to find a way out of this one.

I pretended not to see them, and strolled on. The voyage was agonising. Soon after we were underway one of the younger men came and began making what passed for small talk, but was much more. Jane Carlton swung into action. He began asking about property prices in Sydney, to which I mumbled something vague. I was smoking Marlboro Red cigarettes, and he asked me how much they cost in Sydney. I hadn't lived in Australia since 1978 and had not the slightest idea. It showed. I managed to extricate myself from him but with a feeling of doom. The questioning had been aggressive and these men weren't going to go away.

Then, a welcome flash of inspiration. The Mataram backpackers were getting off at Komodo Island. I had bought a ticket to Flores, but it was also good for Komodo. I would wait until the last passengers were disembarking and get off too. I could hide out there, to work out the next steps.

It worked, but the move had only bought time and I was in misery. In the brief diary entry I made in a cabin on Komodo that night, I calculated chances of reaching Santana at around 55–60 per cent, with my money almost spent and the time on my eight-week tourist visa running out. I wondered where Tommy was—there hadn't been a sign of him since Surabaya, and his company would be welcome.

Morning brought guided tours to see the legendary carnivorous dragons, a hair-raising business once the nature of the beasts was understood. The island was classified by UNESCO as a world heritage site, but had seen better days.

It was inhabited by deer that were attacked regularly by the dragons, but left to limp around with bloody wounds exposed and untreated because there was no qualified veterinarian or wildlife expert on the island. We were accompanied by park rangers equipped with flimsy forked sticks to hold the dragons back if they became aggressive. At certain points on the way to the main viewing post we had to edge past them: the largest were approaching three metres long. The guides had herded the tourists to the best viewing spots, where they watched safely from behind fences. Freshly slaughtered whole goats were thrown to the prehistoric monsters, which ripped the carcasses apart and fought over the spoils in a clash of titans.

There was a television crew filming there, New Zealanders who were making a documentary on their mating habits for Discovery Channel. They didn't mind chatting, partly because a single komodo copulation sometimes lasted days so their work could be boring, subject matter apart. They had to be alert, however. The director told me that when the shoot began they had set up a scene on the beach, coaxing the dragons to it with pieces of raw chicken. They ate the chicken but then turned on him and another member of the crew, chasing them to the end of the pier, 'Why didn't you jump off and swim clear?' I asked. 'Because they can swim,' he replied, pointing to distant Goat Island, to which he said they swam regularly to supplement their diet.

Such was my feeling of isolation at that time that I was tempted to tell them I was a journalist on assignment, and talk about the planned visit to the East Timor mountains—maybe they would invite a fellow hack for a beer. I could not risk it.

I hired a local fisherman to sail me over to Flores, thereby avoiding travel on the rostered Komodo–Flores ferry in case my pursuers were watching the disembarking passengers. It was a flimsy craft, the deck of which seemed to float just above water when we were on the open sea, but the five-hour sail under blazing sun was relaxing. I could almost imagine I was a real tourist.

We docked at Labuanbajo, a fishing village with a tranquil south-sea island quality, set round several coves. The sight of the locals squatting in the marketplace, with their gaudy woven cloths and betel-nut-stained mouths, triggered a twinge of excitement. They were so like the Timorese. They too cultivated and esteemed pigs—lines of tiny piglets trotting along behind a giant sow gave me a sense of homecoming, as did the fighting cocks groomed for their big moment in the ring, tail feathers a mix of shiny reds, blacks and greens. The Wallace Line was about more than fauna—monotheism had given way to animism (despite a veneer of Christianity, as in Timor, the Florinese combine Catholic liturgies with animal sacrifices). The similarities weren't all coincidental, as Flores had been part of Portugal's colonial empire in this region, until a greedy governor had sold it to the Dutch for a mess of florins. Timor was only an island-hop away now, which felt good, despite the ongoing problems.

The village's simplicity was offset by the presence of a large army base at one end with an aggressive blood-and-guts mural at the entrance to remind locals the monotheists were at least still watching. The hanging judge just might have stopped off here. I needed to get off the street quickly, find accommodation and lie low. A Chinese guest-house costing $1.50 a night nestling against the village's small mosque seemed too humble to demand passport registration. It didn't, and was a place for out-of-towners attending religious ceremonies. $1.50 bought a tiny, shabby cubicle, unventilated except for a paneless window with no mosquito netting.

On the night of the 26th I was optimistic in my diary. On condition that I could throw off any pursuers, I upgraded my chances of reaching Santana to 60–70 per cent, adding that my room 'looks like rat country', but that a bottle of cold Bintang beer would brace me for the night.

The next entry at daylight on the 27th told of a sleepless night 'characterised by copulating cats, rampaging rats and a gentleman snoring loudly through the paper-thin partition with the next room'.

Soon after turning off the lights, the rats had begun their activity and I had no hope of sleep for fear one would jump on the bed. They were operating a Ho Chi Minh trail around the perimeter of the cubicle, with its logistic centre in the holed flooring right under the bed. I confirmed they were rats, not mice, early in the evening, when a snout emerged from the corner contiguous with my bed-head. I had already begun drawing the bedclothes into the centre and gripping a torch in one hand ready to flash at trouble-spots, and it withdrew rapidly when I trained the light on it. Later I caught the back of another in the beam through a hole in the floorboard. I glimpsed long, coarse hair. If there had been any sleep possible, it was ruled out by the mosque's multi-decibel speaker system calling the faithful to prayer at 4.30 am. Dawn was welcome when it came an hour later.

I blotted out the rodent nightmare by thinking of Mrs Forbes. Lying alone and helpless in a malarial fever in the foothills of Dili, sliding in and out of delirium, she too had faced rats. She recorded:

> I had gradually drawn almost every article in the hut within my bed. The rats, which at first confined their revels to the darkness of night, got so bold in the unbroken stillness that even in the day-time they tried to gnaw through my bed-curtains, within which books and boots and food had to be secured.[5]

Her greatest fear, she wrote, was that Henry would return from his expedition to find she had been eaten altogether by them.

With a choice between running into the Indonesian secret police and co-habiting with rats, I opted to spend the next day waiting in the rodent-ridden cubicle until the scheduled 5 pm departure of a bus for Ende, 300 km east, from where a ferry sailed to Kupang. The driver who sold the ticket earlier said the bus left 'between 5 and 6', but I arrived to find it had left an hour earlier. Two provisional times had been given, by different sources, for the Ende–Kupang ferry's departure, 6 pm on the 28th and the same time on the 29th. The majority seemed to think it was the latter, and I hoped fervently they were right, because making the connection was essential—both money and visa time were running perilously low.

The disaster of the missed bus gave an opportunity to seek a rat-free *losmen*. There was a bayside guest-house near the bus stop run by a smiling extended family who looked like they had walked out of a Gauguin painting. A rat assessment mission showed the place to be cleaner, but the rooms all had interconnected rafters and gutters (albeit clean concrete ones) running to the exterior, so there were probably some, but they were unlikely to turn on a second Big Night Out. Soon after daybreak, one dared to step gingerly onto a rafter above the bed, but retreated under my aggressive glare. I felt I had earnt my rat-tamer stripes.

After the announcement of various false departure times, the bus finally left at 9.30 am on the 28th. First stop was the highlands town of Ruteng. The Portuguese had not named the island Flores, meaning 'flowers', for nothing. It was rich in flora then, and as we progressed across the island, I imagined how it might have been when they first stepped ashore. Little different, perhaps, as much of it was still unspoilt jungle; I counted papaya trees, bananas, sago, maize (though this was an import from South America), abundant honey, from which beeswax was produced, coffee, tobacco, sandalwood, cinnamon, cloves, lontar palms giving oil and housing materials, sweet potato, limes, coconuts, tamarinds (also imported, from Macassan traders), luxuriant waratah bushes, bougainvillea and frangipani.

As we climbed towards Ruteng, we came across Florinese striding along the roadside in striking black-based *ikat* sarongs, carrying fighting cocks or farm produce, daggers protruding from belts. Poor by conventional standards, these people's lives were culturally rich: even the snottiest-nosed child wore an individually-woven sarong decorated with mystical animist symbols.

A colourful chap boarded the bus with two handsome cockerels—not carried in the special baskets reserved for their class, which button over the bird's back and have a convenient hole out of which the tail plumes are draped languorously to highlight their colours—but clutched in his arms. Each had a string around one leg which was then tied to the seat base to avoid adventurous activity, but one crowed a defiant cock-a-doodle-doo every time the bus stopped and started, which was about every five to ten minutes.

On arrival three of the long-distance passengers left, leaving me as the only remaining contender for Ende. The driver announced he would travel the rest 'tomorrow'. I railed at the deceitfulness of his company but he was unmoveable and bought my silence with a refund. I sat myself in the centre of the town square to negotiate prices for the charter of a *bemo*[6] to Bajawa, half-way to Ende, from which I could catch a connecting bus at 7 am the next day to get there by midday.

My determination to continue at all costs led me to abandon caution and I hired the vehicle of four dubious-looking young louts, having beaten their asking price down from 300,000 rupiahs to 65,000. Further down the road the driver announced he'd left his licence at home and must return. They wanted more money. By now it was getting dark and rainy and my desperation was increasing. They accosted another driver, who said he wouldn't do it for less than 100,000. I offered him 80,000 and he agreed, but now the louts wanted the job after all and a tug-of-war for my custom began. I had committed an error of judgement, and it was imperative to free myself from them. They would probably decide it was easier to drive some of the way and rob me than drive me to Bajawa. I paid them 10,000 to go away.

The substitute driver was an older man called Jam, travelling with one younger companion, Chris. He was around 40, with a Zapata moustache and a winning smile. We had no common language except our humanity. We set off along a road that at times was little better than a jungle track, at first playing the usual *bemo* disco medleys at full blast. He wanted to know if I had a cassette, so we played The Platters singing 'Red Sails in the Sunset', 'The Great Pretender' and 'The Power of Love', which were received with some bemusement. I indicated it was their turn, and he put on a cassette he had recorded of singers from the highlands Mangarrai clan, incantations and chants accompanied by drums, jew's harp and a stringed, violin-type instrument. To the light of a gibbous moon and the strains of this other-wordly music we hurtled on through the jungle. There were occasional settlements along the way and, in between, people walking with torches or burning sticks. A party of deer-hunters carrying flaming brands and hand-carved wooden spears appeared briefly in the headlights.

At one point we stopped at the house of a friend of Jam to collect a flask of hot sweet coffee, which we drank contentedly as we shared a common stock of clove cigarettes. The *losmens* at Bajawa were all booked out when we arrived towards midnight. In the last one we tried, there was a card game in progress among a group of kindly, English-speaking Mangarrais, including a person from Jam's village. I pleaded with them to find me any space to sleep just till leaving for the bus at 5.30 am and a young man generously offered to share his neighbour's room and give me his.

I arrived in Ende at 11.30 am on 29 July, and discovered that the ferry for Kupang was scheduled to leave the next morning. By now there was no sign of INTEL agents and I felt confident to continue.

Ende had once been an interesting historic town but it had suffered an earthquake a few years before and been rebuilt in hideous taste. I booked into The Nirvana Beaming Inn, which was neither nirvana nor beaming, and had a close examination of the spreading itchy rash on my body. At first I thought it was an allergy, but it then occurred that, having encountered so many other vermin on the way, cockroaches and rats for example, I might have parasites on my skin as well. A chemist confirmed my worst fear—I was covered in skin lice, otherwise known as scabies. The infestation began from my elbows, and could thus be traced back to the opera-box-style velvet armrests on the Labuanbajo bus. The pharmacist prescribed a pomade. It killed them and gave temporary relief, but they laid their eggs in the seams of clothes, and unless all garments affected were boiled, they would hatch again in a few days. How could I boil my clothes while constantly on the move, trying to remain invisible in hotels slept in for the shortest possible time? Victory was in sight, but things looked like becoming uncomfortable in the meantime.

I telephoned Zely in Jakarta and organised the Kupang meeting with Tommy, after which F.F. would join us, bringing a new payment I had transferred from Portugal. With a little over a fortnight left on my visa and a dwindling supply of rupiahs, I sailed from Flores for the island of Timor.

5
Near but Far

Kupang to Suai, 30 July – 10 August 1994

I sailed under the guiding eye of Suharto and his vice-president Try Sutrisno, whose portraits hung over the entrance to the VIP compartment occupied by a platoon of soldiers. By 4 am the next day the coastline of Timor was in view.

I booked into a medium-priced hotel on the Kupang beachfront, but to my horror not only was showing my passport unavoidable, but there was a whiteboard in the lobby where they wrote my name in large letters, as they did with all the guests. It would take just one well-informed INTEL agent to walk in at the wrong moment and all would be lost. The only way I could get the name off the board was to check out again as soon as was decent and move to a place at the back of town.

Kupang had an ugly feeling about it. It was the base for the West Timorese territorial Battalion 743, active in the counter-insurgency campaigns on the other side of the island, and a major logistics support centre. It was a relatively large city, and was used as a resort by a crowd of low-life Australians involved in prostitution, drugs and paedophilia—a compatriot who crossed them had been murdered not long before. The guidebook warned that groping foreign women in the street was a favourite occupation of the local youth, and a hit-and-run breast-grabber drove the message home soon after arrival. I walked with a rolled-up newspaper in hand after that, watching the street ahead carefully. Worst of all, the city was seething with secret police.

I found Tommy without much difficulty, but it was impossible to talk along the beach promenade that was our contact point. Men with Ray-Ban shades and clipped moustaches, who I came to think of as 'Tonton Macoutes' after their Haitian namesakes cruised closely by on motorbikes each time we met.[7] Spooked, we decided to move on to So'e, the next town to the east. We telephoned Zely to pass on word to F.F. when he rang in. He was already travelling towards us from Jakarta.

It was in So'e that we met the colourful Andre, owner of a small *losmen*. The atmosphere in the town was different from that in Kupang. So'e was a rural society similar to many towns on the East Timorese side of the border, with the exception that there was a spasm of paramilitary activity underway in preparation for national day on 17 August. School children drilled by army officers marched ceaselessly up and down to the sound of patriotic tunes.

There were a few tourists passing through, the average collection of backpackers, plus a few Dutch people who had lived here before independence. I struck up a conversation with the daughter of Protestant missionaries who was born in So'e, had left as a child and was returning to explore her roots. Many Dutch were only then coming to terms with the events of World War II and its aftermath. They had not been much better as colonisers than the Portuguese, differing merely in style. Under the Japanese occupation the wave of hatred that erupted when their rule collapsed was encouraged and orchestrated. One wing of the nationalist movement collaborated with the Japanese in the interests of eventually expelling their colonial masters. Dutch citizens were interned, tortured, executed, and some women forced to serve in Japanese army brothels as so-called comfort women. The futile police action to restore Dutch rule after the Japanese surrender was unpopular with Holland's Western allies and simply deepened the rancour. It had taken time and the unprejudiced curiosity of a new generation in Holland, expressed in a spate of truth-telling books, for healing to begin.

Andre's *losmen* was off the main road, and nobody bothered us there. Finally, it seemed all the elements were falling into place for the interview with Santana. It only remained for us to meet up with F.F.

On 1 August I wrote: 'Getting closer ... the effort of looking like an enthusiastic tourist gets harder by the day. But will keep beaming for the last stretch, and try to stop scratching.'

After we had booked into our respective rooms, Tommy returned to Kupang to wait for F.F. I felt confident but was worried that the time available to complete my work was dwindling. I needed to catch the boat back to Flores from Kupang by 10 August in order to get back over the border before my tourist visa expired. I resolved to be disciplined and patient, carefully eking out the few remaining rupiahs and keeping out of officialdom's way until F.F. arrived. Andre's establishment was amusingly colourful, with its painted statues and apartment built in the shape of a warship, but it was not a model of hygiene and the nights were cold because So'e is on a plateau. I recorded:

> No rats, but I'm starting to act like an old tramp. I went and bought newspapers to sleep on over the mattress, which I fear is lousy. The sheets were unspeakable so I also bought some lengths of cloth to serve as sheets, first putting down paper, then a layer of foam rubber from my pack, then the sheets. There is a blanket but I'm not touching it as I have very few clothes that aren't infested, so, as it's cold here, I put on layers of them and got in, but there are holes in the wall and chinks in the window, so it was freezing and I woke up with a cold as well as scabies. Oh dear!

By 3 August there was no sign of either Tommy or F.F. There were only seven days to find Santana and return for the boat. In a gesture of ongoing patience, I accompanied the missionaries' daughter and family on a day trip to Niki Niki, an unspoilt West Timorese community, where we hired a guide who showed us the graves of the last kings of Amanuban. The entire royal family, around 20 people, had immolated itself in the late 19th century in preference to submitting to Dutch rule. Close by was a hamlet where people live in the traditional beehive-shaped huts, curious buildings like igloos. I noted in my diary:

> The only outward opening is the door, and fires are lit inside to cook food, provide warmth, dry maize and repel mosquitos. The interior is black with tars, but it looks comfortable otherwise. The Indonesian government has tried to ban these structures on health grounds since the 1970s and force people to live in government-funded concrete houses with corrugated iron roofs. Their response is to move into the 'official' houses and then build a traditional one at the back door. Although the West Timorese have shown no signs of imitating their eastern brothers in a political movement for independence, cultural resistance to their Javanese overlords is pronounced.

Tommy was two days overdue by 5 August, and my rations were down to three chocolate biscuits, a hand of bananas and a bottle of cordial with just enough money to pay that day's rent. Then his smiling face appeared at breakfast. He had good news from recent contacts with the guerrillas, who were certainly expecting us soon, but he had failed to locate F.F. He went off to find him again, and again failed to return.

There was an old man who sold *ikat* weavings regularly at the *losmen* door. They were of fine quality and I sometimes looked over them and admired them, but made clear I couldn't afford to buy anything. In this period of low ebb waiting for Tommy's return with F.F., he came up to me and offered me a gift, smiling and nodding sympathetically. Perhaps he sensed my despair. It was an amulet, a tiny naïve carving of a man's head wrought in deer-horn. I tucked it into my jeans pocket and gave him a good smile back.

When Tommy still didn't return I feared for my sanity, but a renewed call to Zely in Jakarta yielded the message: sit tight, they're coming.

After F.F.'s initial anger when we met, arising from his belief we had failed to keep a rendezvous (when in fact Zely had misled him about *which* Jalan Kartini we were living in—So'e, not Kupang), we were in a celebratory mood. With the money F.F. had brought, we had a good meal together and settled our bills with Andre. They then saw me onto the bus to Atambua, just west of the border, from where I would change in the early hours of the morning for the bus to Suai on the south coast of East Timor, a town I had known well in 1975.

I clutched a letter written to Father Hilário Madeira, the Catholic priest there who was a resistance supporter. It asked him to drive me to the mountains immediately for handover to guerrilla representatives, who would take me to Nino Konis Santana.

The way I saw it panning out was this: on arrival in Atambua, sometime after midnight, there would be a wait of about four hours for the Suai bus. Atambua being a large district capital, I figured there would be a fairly busy terminal where I could buy coffee, food if I was lucky, and find a spot to rest. Being a foreigner entering Suai alone could be a problem. There would undoubtedly be a significant Indonesian military presence, as it too was an important town. However, I had taken comfort from the *Lonely Planet*, which treated it as though it was on the backpacker route, and said there were a couple of *losmens* there. It had been right so far. I didn't think it would be thronged with foreigners, but I hoped their presence wouldn't be unusual and that one or two might even be around to provide cover. I assumed that, in any case, Father Hilário should be able to get me out of town soon after arrival, or hide me safely until we could travel.

When the bus drew into Atambua at about 1 am, the town was at rest and there was barely a light visible. As is customary in Third World countries, the driver offered an individualised service to each passenger's door. Some went to hotels, others to private homes, then there was me … 'Just drop me at the bus terminus please,' I said in a matter-of-fact voice. It drew up at a bleak, ill-lit concrete shelter full of sleeping Timorese peasants and their animals, including an old lady with a bronchial chest cuddling a noisy pig. My arrival caused a stir. People sat up and stared, talked loudly about the meaning of it all. Not wishing to draw attention to myself I stretched out on a concrete bench away from the light, drawing a sarong over my body until not a centimetre of white skin was visible. They quietened down, and I slid into an enjoyable slumber, to be woken sometime later by the awareness of two lights advancing among the sleeping figures, in my direction. They stopped at my bench. Peeping under the sarong I saw a pair of shiny black military boots. They were joined to a pale-complexioned Javanese policeman with close-cropped hair. He had a large flashlight and an even larger truncheon, and was accompanied by another. He spoke halting English and asked me what I was doing. I explained I was travelling to meet some Australian friends in Suai, and had just a few hours more to wait for the connecting bus. 'We go to *pos*!' he said, unsmilingly.[8] Was this an arrest? I pretended I thought he was suggesting I should go and sleep at the police station for safety. 'Oh, I'm fine here thank you, officer. Don't want to miss my bus. The people here are so nice, I'm absolutely safe thank you,' I burbled, with a sweeping gesture towards my fellow travellers, their pigs and cockerels. He repeated what appeared to be a command, even more sternly: 'We go to *pos* to sleep!' My journey seemed to be at an end. Then he said goodbye, turned on his heels and went off with his mate. It seemed he had been trying to say that he and his colleague were off to bed.

When the bus crossed into East Timor the next morning I experienced a surge of elation, which turned quickly into sadness for all that had passed and been lost in those 19 long years. So many people dead. Many of the passengers were East Timorese who were watching me curiously. It was a standard brightly-coloured *bemo* packed with parcels and animals as well as people. The window panes were of smoked glass except for one clear strip at eye level, which I hoped would offer disguise from any Indonesians looking in. None were travelling on the bus. I slumped low in the seat and trained my gaze through the smoked glass. I knew I would have to be visible sooner or later, but wanted to minimise those occasions. However, as we drew near Suai, the bus stopped and let on two Indonesian policemen who looked closely over the passengers then took seats down the back, before alighting 3 km further down the road.

I had visited Suai on my first trip to what was then Portuguese Timor in April 1975 and associated it with the classical forms of Timorese culture. It had left a strong impression. Our group was escorted into the town by warriors on horseback, heads wrapped in bright turbans, large gold medallions at their breast. Seated cross-legged under a scorching sun, we watched women with the red, black, yellow and pink sarongs of Suai wheel and sway to an ascending drumbeat, mimicking the motions of an eagle on the wing. The town had an aristocratic air, which showed in the proud gait of its inhabitants. The abundant rainfall of the south coast lowlands made it relatively prosperous, giving two rice harvests a year, and its rulers were of the powerful Tetum-speaking Belu kingdom from which the East Timorese draw their national identity. They speak classical

Tetum, known as Tetum Terik, not the bastardised form of the language spoken in Dili.

I knew, in theory, what to expect in terms of the everyday changes effected by Indonesian rule from the hundreds of distressed letters smuggled from the territory I had read and the interviews conducted with refugees. But if my head was prepared for it, my heart wasn't: the first hours in the territory were a cultural shock. The roads under Indonesian rule were much better. Under the Portuguese colonial administration they were almost non-existent, and road travel in 1975 had been a prolonged, bone-rattling nightmare. The general appearance of the town as we approached it seemed little changed. However, as we entered and I saw more, my heart sank. I tried to keep my head down and not stare too much, but I was able to glimpse an Indonesian command-post on a hill to the left as we entered, with the red and white flag of the Republic of Indonesia fluttering above. For many years there had been no fighting in Suai itself, and only limited guerrilla activity in the surrounds, but the base was bristling with activity. Muscular Indonesian officers, mostly Javanese in appearance, with close-cropped hair, efficient-looking and combat-ready, were bustling around speaking into walkie talkies or driving in and out in Land Rovers. For some reason the film *The Young Lions* came to mind and, high on the hill, they seemed as foreign, separate and offensive as the Nazis must have seemed in occupied Europe.

Two forlorn squads of high school children were drilling for national day under the barked commands of Indonesian soldiers. All along the archipelago, householders were obliged to paint their front fences and hang out the national flag, while school children were engaged in a frenzy of endless marching to patriotic songs. It was like a throwback to eastern Europe in Stalin's time but, in truth, the school kids in West Timor and other areas seemed to enter into it with gusto, happy young pioneers against a sunset sky. The East Timorese children were grimly expressionless. Perhaps the soldiers shouting at them had killed or tortured their parents or their uncles, aunts, brothers or sisters. 1975 and the hope of democracy belonged to a very distant past.

On the individualised service principle, the bus driver asked me where I wanted to be dropped off. '*Gereja*,' I replied, using the Indonesian word for church. It was a considered choice designed to send a signal to any Timorese nationalists on board (probably 95 per cent of the passengers, given the crusading human rights role of the Catholic church), but it also made sense to seek Father Hilário first thing instead of alighting in the town centre. I could move quickly from bus to church building almost unobserved. It wheeled first into the town square to drop other passengers. I then realised that the dark glass offered no screen, because a man spotted my white face and began calling to me through the window. He was a ruddy-faced European of about 60 with long white hair, unkempt beard, and just a sprinkling of teeth. '*Fala Portugûes? Fala Portugûes?*' ('Do you speak Portuguese?') he kept shouting excitedly. I shrugged my shoulders in incomprehension, saying 'Can you speak English please?' There was no way I would speak Portuguese here. He withdrew, disappointed. Years later I met him again in Dili and heard his story. Known as Master Cruz, he was a Portuguese marine who had accidentally been left behind by the Portuguese army when it withdrew in December 1975, and had found himself stranded in Indonesian-occupied Timor. This latter-day Ancient Mariner button-holed the few Westerners who turned up in the territory to tell his story and seek news from the outside world.

There were no other foreigners in town. Not a backpacker in sight—two out of three of my assumptions had been wrong so far. This meant that the two *losmens* described by my guidebook would most likely be tenanted exclusively by the Indonesian military.

A young Timorese nun answered the door when I called in at the church residence. Father Hilário had gone to Dili, she told me, and was expected back soon. This was a blow. I needed to speak to him personally, I explained, as I had news to convey from a mutual friend I had come across in Kupang. She looked upset at this dilemma, but could offer no solution. As though inhabiting the era of Mrs Forbes, I pointed out that I was a single woman travelling alone, and would not feel secure sleeping in one of the *losmens*, modesty demanding a more sheltered situation—would the church have accommodation? (Mrs Forbes would have been scornful of such wimpishness.) She replied that there were some Filipina nuns from the Carmelite order nearby who might help. I found them and introduced myself as Jane Carlton, spinning the 'Father Hilário's mutual friend from Kupang' story. I requested a bed until he returned and they assented.

The nuns suggested I should try ringing the priest in Dili to inform him I was there. One offered to accompany me to Suai post office. The phones were inside the building, in a row opposite the main counter, which was staffed entirely by uniformed Indonesians. After we booked the call one of the staff indicated the phone it would come through on. As it rang and I lifted the receiver, he simultaneously lifted a receiver behind the counter, with no attempt to disguise the action, and remained with it glued to his ear throughout our conversation. This was in Portuguese, so it was not terribly useful to him, and besides I spoke in guarded euphemisms. Father Hilário made clear that he had been aware of my imminent arrival from Father Domingos Soares, and had been driving back to Suai the day before when a distressing problem arose. He had knocked an INTEL agent off his motorbike, injuring him slightly. As a result the

Indonesian army was attempting to extort a million rupiahs from him and he couldn't return to Suai until the matter was settled. This wasn't as much as it sounded—at that time around US$120—but I gathered that the occupation authorities knew of his pro-resistance activities, so his situation was delicate. They could press charges against him, and even trump up extra accusations (Father Soares had been falsely accused of murdering a fellow Timorese in a bid to neutralise him). But he urged me to stay where I was and promised to come as soon as possible, saying he thought he would resolve the matter soon.

As I sat down to the evening meal one of the Carmelites said to me: 'You must go and register at the police station tomorrow. The authorities saw you arrive in town, you know.' It was a jolt. We had chatted earlier about the situation in Suai, and I had assumed that any religious order working here could not help but sympathise with the Timorese church position. When I had asked whether there was a mosque in Suai—out of curiosity, since there was only one mosque in all Timor in 1975, for the less than a thousand practising Muslims—the same nun had pointedly replied, 'Yes, but it's only for the foreigners.' That was the only indication they might be taking a stand against the occupation, but it could equally be explained by religious prejudice against Islam. I did not reply to her demand for the time being. Best to get her alone to explain there would be no registering at the police station. The chance came early next morning walking alone alongside her as we went to breakfast. 'I'm afraid there are reasons I can't register at the police station,' I said. She spun round, her face white. 'Why? Who are you?' she asked. 'I'm sorry, but I can't tell you. I'll leave now.' 'In any case, you must register,' she insisted, 'but I'll arrange for you to register with the Kepala Desa (town mayor) rather than the police.' This official was apparently Timorese, so it was just acceptable under the circumstances, if not desirable.

After breakfast I wrote a hurried note to Father Hilário. I had consulted *Lonely Planet* and selected the name of a *losmen* in Atambua, the Timor Raya. I explained that I had to return to Atambua because of the insistence that I register with authorities, which raised the risk of arrest. Would it be possible for him to collect me at the Timor Raya as soon as he returned, as my visa was running out and I needed to travel urgently to the mountains? (Atambua is only around 40 km from Suai on the other side of the border, and there was regular traffic between the two towns, so this was feasible.) I sealed it, returned to the Timorese nun at the church, and begged her to ensure he received it on return.

The Carmelite drove me to the Kepala Desa's office. He was out, and in my last act in the guise of Jane Carlton I scrawled that name and a Sydney address in the book, before continuing in their car to the bus station. I was not well-disposed to them, so muttered a cursory farewell. Tommy's face appeared among the boarding passengers. We glanced silently at each other. At least he was there and aware of what was happening. He walked past to a back seat, then got off the bus a few kilometres down the road. Before it started again, he came to my window saying some phrase that I couldn't hear. In truth I didn't want him to be talking to me publicly, but I had to acknowledge him, and said, 'Louder, I can't hear you.' He was still uttering that unknown phrase that sounded like 'Java' as we roared off. There was a restaurant near the Atambua bus terminus called Warung Java and I looked for him there several times after arrival, in vain.

I booked in at the Timor Raya on the morning of 10 August, the day I had planned to leave Timor from Kupang after interviewing Santana. I had nine days left on my visa. The strategic retreat to Atambua had been successful, but what were the chances of still seeing the guerrilla commander now? A miracle would be needed to save the venture.

By the next afternoon despair was kicking in and the empty packets of *kreteks* were piling up. Lying listening to round-the-clock BBC broadcasts in an Atambua flophouse was not bringing success any nearer. Then at 3 pm there was a gentle tap on the door. I opened it to see Domingos Soares, the man they called 'Father Maubere, the nationalist priest'.[9] 'My car's round the corner. Can you meet me there in half an hour?' he asked.

6
With the Guerrillas

Lete-foho 11-13 August 1994

The young priest, who I had met previously in Portugal and admired greatly, used a battered four-wheel-drive vehicle for the rounds of his parish, covering vast distances in the mountains. He had curly hair and an irrepressibly sunny disposition, although his daily work gave little cause for happiness. It was mainly tending torture victims, caring for newly widowed women and their children, and confronting the Indonesian military to free prisoners or complain over their worst human rights abuses. It was a risky business and the priests themselves were sometimes detained or beaten for the positions they took. Since 1975 the Catholic church had seen an upsurge in nominal believers; under the Indonesian system citizens were obliged to register their religious faith, choosing from Islam, Christianity, Buddhism or Hinduism, and there was a stampede to register as Christians because of the protection it afforded. Animism was not an option, although it represented the real world-view of the majority of Timorese, with a mixture of Christian saints and liturgy thrown in for good measure. His popularity and uncompromising defence of his flock meant Indonesian authorities no longer tangled lightly with Domingos Soares. Because of Father Hilário's current problems with authorities, Soares had decided to take over from him and assist me himself.

He put me in the passenger seat next to him, lowered it to an almost horizontal position, and gave me a floppy hat to put over my face. 'Pretend you're asleep, and I'll do the rest,' he said. We had to pass through various Indonesian roadblocks in daylight, and he warned me when each was approaching. He travelled these roads regularly, and with a few words in Indonesian and a wave of the hand, he sailed through unchallenged with his mysterious passenger.

We travelled a different route from the one I would have taken from Suai with the other priest. We were heading for Dili (which I had been reluctant to pass through previously, because my face was familiar to many people there).

This way involved driving from Atambua to the border post at Batugadé, through Balibo, and then along a secondary road over the mountains to Dili, from a turn-off at the Nunura river. I could not resist peeping at certain points—at Batugadé, where I had experienced my baptism of fire in September 1975, and then at Balibo, where five colleagues had been gunned down by Indonesian special forces a month later. It was remarkably unchanged, sickeningly familiar. It triggered a sensation of dread.

From the fleeting glimpses I allowed myself, it was clear that many of the other villages we drove through had been transformed, Indonesianised beyond recognition. Blocks of shanty houses had sprung up with no reference to traditional Timorese values, as well as ugly concrete houses with corrugated iron roofs. The outskirts of Dili resembled the slums of Jakarta, and at every turn there were foreign soldiers.

In Dili the priest drove straight into the São José seminary, where he had some tasks to complete before continuing. From there we went to eat at the restaurant of Olandina Alves, a woman who had been a friend in 1975. I remembered her as an enthusiastic young FRETILIN militant in the tight bell-bottomed jeans of that year. We embraced, and she gave a brief account of her life since then. She had been an announcer for the nationalists' radio station in Dili during the period of FRETILIN rule. When Indonesian troops landed they abducted her to Kupang and forced her to become a latter-day 'Tokyo Rose', broadcasting anti-FRETILIN propaganda for the Suharto regime. Her husband had been killed in the fighting, and she was pregnant with his child. She had the baby alone in Kupang and suffered several years of hardship, misery and humiliation before she was allowed to return to her homeland. In recent years she had been elected a deputy in the Indonesian-installed regional parliament in Dili. Although she represented Megawati Sukarnoputri's opposition PDI party, Timorese who didn't know her history saw her as a collaborationist. Behind the scenes she worked for the resistance and had recently opened the restaurant in a secluded site accessible to resistance operatives. She served simple Portuguese-style food accompanied by rough red wine or local beer on tables covered with red gingham cloths.

Night had fallen when we resumed the journey. Father Domingos talked his way through several roadblocks. I had no idea where in the mountains we were. The night was a moonless pitch black, but occasionally my eye caught the shiny leaves of coffee trees, which suggested the Ermera district. After almost two hours' driving he spoke: 'I'm going to leave you in the hands of some other people soon. They will take you to the Comandante. You can trust them completely.' Further down the road he suddenly swung right and entered the driveway of a country house at high speed, drawing up close to the front door. It swung open and he bundled me out, into the waiting hands of someone who pulled me inside and slammed the door shut behind us. The priest reversed and sped away.

I calculated the time to be about midnight. Inside the house was a woman and her husband, both in their late 30s or early 40s. They grasped my hands in greeting, whispering in Portuguese, 'Good evening, good evening, welcome!' The interior revealed a Timorese household identical to those I'd known many years before. With a floor of beaten earth and modest, well-ordered décor highlighting the symbols of their piety, it was illuminated with a kerosene lamp and candles. There was a small family altar with a crucifix and a poster of Pope John Paul II on the wall. The tables were covered with white doilies.

There was an enamel washstand with warm water and a hand-towel to freshen up. They showed me where the *mandi* was, and a bamboo bed, before serving a small supper they had prepared. 'You must rest a little,' the woman said, 'at 3 am you will leave with my husband. We will wake you.' They did so punctually, with a hot coffee at the ready. They led me to the back of the house, where there was a small motorbike. The man pulled a balaclava over his head, straddled it and gunned the engine. When it was revving satisfactorily he gestured for me to get on behind and grip his waist. He told me to keep my white hands under his jacket, because if we passed an Indonesian military vehicle they could be picked up in the headlights. I could hide my face in his shoulder.

We travelled along a heavily wooded bitumen road for some time without encountering any traffic. Then a car came into view, parked on the shoulder of the road. He drew up behind it, and the priest's face appeared briefly in the lights. They spoke together in rapid Tetum, and then we continued at the same cautious pace, for another quarter of an hour or so before he pulled off the road into a clearing, hiding the bike under some bushes. He told me to sit firm, out of view of the road, and wait. He would return.

I took cover under the bushes in this dark, silent place. The minutes ticked on and still he didn't come. My nerve failed temporarily, and I lost all perspective. The blood was whooshing in my ears, vision confused. In panic I shuffled rapidly up the hillside further back from the road, distant from where he had left me. I heard feet approaching, and tried to remember what he looked like. His face had become featureless in my memory, and I could not recall the sound of his voice—I had, after all, only been with him for little more than an hour. What if it was an Indonesian coming? Was I crazy being here? The person was searching the bushes. Then I heard his voice calling '*Está aqui?*' ('Are you here?') and the fear subsided. I replied and came towards him.

I travelled with him only a short distance more. We stopped, left the bike, and began ascending a hill on foot. Two more men came into view, and he took his leave. We continued the ascent. The next hour or so is a blurred dream in my memory as I passed from one group to another on the way up an increasingly steep mountain at forced-march pace. They were all unarmed so, properly speaking, I wasn't yet in the hands of the guerrillas. Struggling to keep up and maintain my footing in the dark, I lost track of how many different people marched with me. Reluctantly I had to ask them to slow down at one point—my heart was working too severely overtime for its health. Finally we reached a small rocky plateau in front of a house. They gestured for me to stay put, and one man remained outside while the others went in. It was a while before they returned. Then they guided me towards the house and ushered me in the door. When my eyes adjusted to the light I saw a group of around six long-haired men with semi-automatic rifles. One stepped forward and asked: 'Jill?'. 'Yes', I replied in Portuguese. 'I'm Konis Santana', he said, and wrapped me in an enormous bear-hug.

The photos I'd seen of him didn't do him justice. They gave an impression of scrawniness. He was a full-faced handsome fellow with a shock of long curly hair and a wispy mandarin-style beard. He moved his hands expressively to orchestrate his words, and had a habit of cocking his head quizzically to one side in conversation, as though buying time to think of his answer. Xanana Gusmão had a similar winning gesture—perhaps it was contagious among guerrilla commanders, or perhaps it was an imitation This was possible, as it later became evident that Santana suffered from an acute sense that he was inadequate for the leadership. It had been thrust on him, just as it had originally been thrust on the now-imprisoned and then exceedingly reluctant Xanana many years earlier, after the death of Nicolau Lobato.

We were not in a military encampment but in a bamboo-and-thatch home in the hamlet of Mirtutu. Although four gunmen watched constantly from behind curtained windows as we spoke, it was the mass of civilians he was living among who were the ultimate guarantors of his security, on Mao Tzedung's maxim of 'living among the people as a fish swims in water'. *Estafetas* (runners, couriers) arrived here daily from all zones of the country with messages for the commander, departing with orders and replies.

Some women brought in coffee, smiling and bowing in greeting. Santana and I were still getting to know each other and were elated at the fact of our meeting. We joked about how Ali Alatas would respond if he knew Indonesia's most wanted journalist was interviewing its most wanted guerrilla. We discussed my program, and I was upset with disappointment to hear that they had planned to escort me on an ambitious tour of resistance bases, which would involve days of marching between them. There were only a few days available altogether, I explained, because it had taken so long to get here. I would have to race to reach the border before my visa expired. But having succeeded once I could return, I promised, this time with a television crew, to do the full tour. We settled for a program of three days.

Above all I wanted to just talk and talk, to learn Santana's personal story and discover what motivated him and the men with him, to gain an accurate assessment of the military situation, including both Indonesian and resistance troop strengths and dispositions, the number of casualties being suffered on both sides, Indonesia's intelligence and military structure, the human rights situation of the civilian population, and his perspectives for the future. Were they receiving the large sums of money people abroad had donated for them since the 1991 Santa Cruz massacre? Were their international representatives supporting them adequately, both in terms of material aid and information? Could they win the war? If not, could the Indonesians still subjugate them after 19 years of successful resistance?

We ended up talking almost non-stop for 48 hours. But first the commander excused himself and suggested I rest while he finished an urgent report. A delegation from the Japanese Diet was arriving in Dili that day, and the document he was writing would be smuggled to them—an *estafeta* was waiting to take it. The sun was just coming up as we parted for a few hours; he descended to his basement hideout to work, while the householders took me to a bedroom. Before we did, I mentioned the need to also take photos in a jungle setting, to which he replied that we would march to a suitable location under cover of night.

After showing me to the room, the woman of the house explained that the lavatory was outside and that when I used it I should cover my head and face to avoid being seen by neighbours. Although Konis Santana was protected by his civilian supporters, only a small elite knew he was there. I agreed to be careful, and seized on the opportunity to finish a piece of urgent business—kill the vermin. I asked if they could please boil all my clothes while I slept, explaining my uncomfortable predicament. They gave me a sarong and took the offending garments, which were returned later in pristine condition, if a little shrunken (by this time they were pretty ragged anyway). I went to sleep to the pleasant buzz of household sounds—children preparing for school and adults for work, the Indonesian radio station from Dili and the cooing and flapping of doves in the rafters.

7
Comandante Nino Konis Santana

When Santana called for me a few hours later he pulled out a bottle, asking, 'Would you like some Portuguese wine? I don't drink myself ...' Sweet innocent! It was a bottle of Johnnie Walker whisky, and a breakfast-time swig was just what a journalist needed to complete her happiness in a guerrilla commander's hideout.

Nino Konis Santana came from the Fataluku tribe, a distinctive people from the eastern Lautem region of East Timor. He was born of a *liurai* (traditional king) in Tutuala on 12 January 1955, which made him 39 at the time of our interview.

Since the war began, leadership of the resistance had been increasingly drawn from fighters born in the eastern regions. Here the people are ethnically closer to the Melanesians of the island of Papua New Guinea and had more to lose by Javanese conquest. Under the 1975 FRETILIN leadership of Nicolau Lobato, Tetum speakers from the central and Dili districts were prominent. By a process of attrition they had been killed or captured during the years. Xanana Gusmão's ascendance set the pattern. He was born in Manatuto, near the eastern capital of Baucau, and after Lobato's death he and surviving guerrillas known as 'the 50 fugitives to the east' broke though an encirclement and fled to the Lospalos region, where they were hidden by the community while they planned the rebirth of the decimated resistance, which Gusmão then led in the field for the next 12 years. By the time of his capture in 1992, most of the senior commanders were easterners—from the wily, beloved David Alex to Sabika, Ular, Falur, Eli Foho Rai Bo'ot and Taur Matan Ruak, as well as Santana. Two other of Gusmão's closest collaborators, Mau Huno and Ma' Hodu, succeeded him in turn as commanders before being captured by the Indonesian army, after which the mantle fell on Santana's shoulders. In taking command Santana was to be the first and only Fataluku to lead the East Timorese resistance, a source of major pride in his region.

His father was polygamous, as was customary, and the family from his mother consisted of three boys and three girls. The two other boys had died since, leaving him as the sole son. 'My father really wanted me to have children,' he said, with a touch of sadness. The *liurai* also had two boys and two girls by his second wife, of which only one daughter and son survived. The old man died of tuberculosis in 1990. Santana had last seen his mother in 1982, when passing through the district on a combat mission; the only news of her since then had come just three days before my arrival when a cousin came to say she was still alive.

He attended primary school at a Catholic mission in Tutuala, then transferred to the Salesian secondary school in nearby Fuiloro. He later studied at their seminary in Baucau before moving to Dili for teacher training. It was there that he had met me in 1975, with students from UNETIM, the newly organised students' union, of which he was a militant. Embarrassingly, he had been part of a large group and I had no memory of him. He had read and been moved by the theorists of the anti-Portuguese colonialist struggle, such as Mozambique's Samora Machel and Guinea-Bissau's Amílcar Cabral. He therefore had a high educational level by Timorese standards of that era, yet he insisted to me that he was 'an illiterate'.

After Gusmão's capture and the quick loss of the two succeeding commanders, there had been a bid by Timorese leaders abroad to direct the conduct of the war in the field, from Europe or New York. (Gusmão continued as nominal supreme commander from his cell in Cipinang prison, which was accepted by all.) In particular, there was a proposal that José Ramos Horta, who led the diplomatic front of the resistance, should become commander in a troika with Gusmão and Santana, because there was no guerrilla qualified to take over altogether. Ramos Horta was respected as a diplomat but had no experience of the military struggle. The move had been defeated, but it seemed Santana had been browbeaten into believing he was an illiterate barbarian because he knew nothing of the subtleties of thinking in foreign chancelries. He was suffering from a crisis of confidence. 'Most of us only have primary school education,' he told me, 'we have no theoretical or cultural conditions—the Indonesians call us "the illiterates".' As well as some of their peers, it seemed. 'Don't you think the fact that you know every inch of this land, and have a close knowledge of the needs of your people, and have their love, is a qualification? Surely book-learning can be had after the war, but these skills are precious?' I asked.

The means they had to fight were miserable, and they had received almost no outside aid. It was a shocking situation because large sums of money had been collected for them in public appeals, particularly in Portugal. Some had been wearing the same clothes for a decade, patched and re-patched. They literally had the arse out of their pants. They spent a large part of their lives marching through difficult jungle but only a few had decent leather boots; most wore rubber boots and some wore thongs, or flip-flops as they are known in Asia.

Of weaponry, there were some decent guns captured from the Indonesians, principally the American-made M16, but some guerrillas were still fighting with ancient Mauser rifles inherited from the Portuguese army (much of their arsenal having been left behind when they abdicated power after their botched decolonisation attempt) or the G3 semi-automatic rifle from the same source. The bullets had long since been exhausted, so they adapted ammunition, of which there was a general shortage, from Indonesian M16s, R15s or Akais.

At times they resorted to traditional weapons. Hakiak, a fine, strong-looking 37-year-old bodyguard from Cailaco was an expert archer, and Santana said he had recently assassinated two Indonesian officers with a bow and arrow as they washed in a stream.

The desired aim was to smuggle arms and ammunition into the country, but if they had funds this wouldn't be necessary. It was relatively easy to buy guns or ammunition from poorly paid Indonesian soldiers, who had no stomach for the war. This way the resistance could have supplemented its stock of captured weapons, but the bitter truth was that they were starved of funds. During my days with Santana I asked to see, where possible, the incoming messages from *estafetas*, and he had shown me reports from his district commanders giving tallies of bullets bought or stolen by villagers for the fighters in the past month—60 in one district, 20 or so in another, moving testimony of the dedication of ordinary people to the guerrilla leadership. All over East Timor men, women and even children were collecting bullets one-by-one at enormous personal risk. The villagers were the only people Santana felt he could rely on but he underlined that the means at their disposal were extremely limited. 'The population supports us, feeds and hides us when they can, but they put their lives at risk because they are always under the watch of INTEL,' he said.

He continued:

> Our logistic problems are the greatest concern ... Many times we have had to suspend operations because we have had nothing to eat. How many of our guerrillas have died trying to survive eating grass and roots, in hiding because the enemy knew our movements? Life is increasingly difficult. So many have died on intelligence missions, communicating between our units. We need means of communication, we've already told our people abroad, but we're still waiting for medium-wave transmitters to communicate between units ... We have to count on capturing Indonesian arms and our blood is spilt in these encounters. This is a very difficult struggle and we can count only on our own forces.[10]

Konis was not well, suffering pain above all from tooth decay acquired during 19 years in the bush, as well as from periodic bouts of malaria. Like many of his men he had unextracted bullets in his body.

Suno Moris, one of his bodyguards who had also protected Xanana, had a record ten bullets lodged in his body. 'Does it ever hurt?' I asked. 'Only sometimes,' he replied, but photos printed on return from Timor showed that his face looked like a mask, as though he was in constant pain.

Suno Moris had a fierce reputation in dealing with Indonesian soldiers who crossed his path. His life had been sad. Born in Balibo, he was eight years old when Indonesian forces landed in Dili, where he had been sent to school. His parents apparently perished in the invasion: he never heard of them again. He had brothers and sisters, but they had been evacuated to Darwin during the civil war and he also knew nothing of them. A year later he went to the mountains, following the guerrillas with the many civilians travelling behind them for protection. By the age of 12 he was a fighter. He described himself as 'self-taught' in weaponry and 'a bachelor and a Catholic'. Like many other Timorese he said that he hated Indonesians despite being a Christian, on the grounds that:

> Portugal was like a father who gave the Timorese the liberty to choose their own future. FRETILIN defended the people and declared independence. Nationally, the Timorese will was for total independence. Indonesia has mass forces and we can't hope to defeat them, but we have organised the means possible to defend ourselves. I don't think of anything else but freedom. I hope that Timor can be free like other nations. I can't think of the future, only the task of freeing Timor.[11]

He had sustained his bullet wounds in a shoot-out with the Indonesian army in 1977.

Santana had copped his six bullets in a 1990 ambush that had left psychological scars as well, because six of his dearest comrades-in-arms, of a unit of eight fighters, had been killed. His own survival resembled a return from the dead. He described how, soon after the visit of Australian trade unionist Robert Domm, the Indonesian army launched a new offensive in which 70–80 guerrillas were killed, over 30 captured and 46 of their weapons seized. His unit was camped on the slopes of Mt Ramelau. Twelve battalions had been deployed in the offensive:

> It was an afternoon of heavy mist, around 5 pm. The ambush surprised us. Six died after a long fight—Miguel, Mau Rui Zacarias, Evaristo, Moises Mau Liko, Moises La Sane and Moises Mau Huno. My friend Kakehe was hit early, first of all in the arm. I lost my gun and was hit in the neck, buttocks and foot. We stumbled out of the area, alone and gravely injured. I had to support Kakehe, hiding and stealing vegetables from people's gardens. He was almost crying from his pain. He had taken shrapnel, and was naked with only his gun. We lived hidden for a month, eating *cami* leaves and *peiju*, as well as maize we stole. We later managed to drag ourselves to the south coast where we found people to hide and look after us.[12]

The experience changed his thinking. 'I realised that the survival of the guerrilla has no guarantees, each individual faces extinction, and our role is to prepare for [our replacement by others],' he recalled.

The fighters were in regular contact with their representatives abroad, but received little response to their requests for material aid. The contrast between their condition and the lives of those in the diplomatic front was glaring. The latter did not necessarily have large cash incomes, and certainly worked hard, but they constantly toured the globe to attend meetings, speaking engagements and UN sessions, travel that was funded by international organisations. Some had diplomatic status, with the benefits that entailed. In short, life on the cocktail-party circuit was as remote from the reality of the military struggle as one could imagine. The irony was that the continued military resistance was their *raison d'être*, and that if it came to a successful conclusion, so would their privileges. This conflict of interests between politicians in exile and the movements they represented was not unique to the Timorese. I had seen it before, in movements such as Namibia's SWAPO, whose leaders lived in Angola during the military struggle.

In our marathon interview, Santana asserted that as we spoke there were between 13 and 15 Indonesian battalions in East Timor, around 9,000 soldiers, apart from paramilitary forces.[13] He described attacks in June by companies from battalions 744 and 723 in the Atabae and Cailaco areas, and said that the Lore rainforest and Iliomar mountain range in the south-east were infested with around 3,000 troops in a current offensive. He had received unconfirmed reports of one or two guerrilla casualties.

Figures on the resistance side were grim. Since the Santa Cruz massacre many persecuted students had applied to join the guerrillas, but there were not enough guns for them, and the FALINTIL policy was to reject them as recruits and ask them to instead remain active on the political front in the towns.

My jaw dropped when he said the number of people they had under arms was now a mere 400–450 (it had never been stated publicly as less than a thousand before), but he hastened to add that they could mobilise an extra thousand if necessary. More than 60 guerrillas had been killed in the past 12 months, he said.

Santana was not despondent, however, and detailed the modest re-organisation he had conducted since taking on the field leadership. East Timor was divided into five military regions, each under a FALINTIL commander and deputy commander who operated autonomously (under Xanana they had been organised in conventional companies). Santana's military chief-of-staff was Taur Matan Ruak, a flamboyant and feared fighter from the Baucau region, who planned operations on a day-to-day basis.[14]

The autonomous structure allowed greater mobility, and had been strengthened by the return to arms of veteran fighter Ernesto 'Dudo' Fernandes in November 1991. A native of the border town of Hatolia, he fled from Indonesian control, taking 120 villagers and four guns, including an M16 given to him by Xanana Gusmão to encourage and honour his return. Some of the villagers were simply looking for sanctuary from the repression that followed the Dili massacre, and 47 later surrendered. Dudo's return to active combat allowed the re-opening of a front in the important northern border region, which he commanded with his nephew Roque (*nom de guerre* Iku Rai Klarun) as deputy. Both Dudo and the youthful Roque were present during my days with Santana, with the veteran commander listing an impressive roll of military actions since his return, including the deaths of two Indonesian officers and one soldier, the wounding of four and the capture of various weapons. Domingos Soares told me later that Dudo was at Santana's base rather than in action because he had been ill. He was 48, bearded, with wild-looking hair (East Timorese do not cut their hair while at war), while Roque, 21, had a bushy Afro haircut and wore a large crucifix around his neck, not merely a cross, but a cross with the body of Jesus hanging from it.

Santana stressed that the conflict was essentially a war of attrition:

> It's impossible to destroy FALINTIL because our base is with the people. An Indonesian defeat is also impossible. We were defeated once, in 1978, after the death of Nicolau Lobato, but we rose from the ashes. The guarantee of FALINTIL's survival lies in our capacity to attack, and we have won this by consolidating our political conditions. Our forces are focused on informing us of the enemy's movements.[15]

He listed their most recent attacks. An operation in the eastern Lospalos sector in June had netted two Belgian-made FNC automatic rifles with moveable stocks; in Vemasse the same month they had killed two Indonesian soldiers and captured an SPS rifle, with a similar attack in Natarbora resulting in one Indonesian death and the capture of another gun of the same make. In Atsabe they had launched a surprise attack on a military base housing battalions 744 and 723, many of whom fled under fire. Four Indonesians were wounded, they claimed.

Santana said also that certain areas of the country were under such secure FALINTIL control that he could live in them openly for weeks at a time.

This information was in stark contrast to the Jakarta-influenced picture being presented in the world press, claiming that armed resistance had long since been quelled and that the Indonesian military was no longer involved in armed activity.

The leader reserved angry words for the Australian government. 'In adopting a position of close support for Indonesia, Australia is insulting the principles of pluralist democracy it claims to uphold,' he asserted. 'It is an extra burden for the resistance, to know that the country closest to us contributes nothing to a solution of the Timor problem. For us, Australia is supporting Indonesia in the extermination of our people.'

There was one final message Nino Konis Santana wanted to drive home: that he was ashamed of human rights violations committed by his movement in the past, and was determined they would never be repeated. He wanted these on record. He spoke of the early days of their struggle, before the 1978 death of Nicolau Lobato, when 'we believed Marxism-Leninism was the remedy for all ills', and claimed that the authority of the first commander had been usurped by a radical wing of the FRETILIN party. 'Nicolau was a real hero, a lion among lions, he had authority over everybody and everything, he had qualities as a military man and as a statesman, but he was forced to choose between the revolutionary way and a normal path. If Nicolau was tough, it was to survive,' he observed. He described how it was not until 1982, when Xanana Gusmão broke with FRETILIN and forged a policy of a national resistance embracing all parties, that the reign of the hard-liners within FRETILIN ended. It continued to be respected as the founding independence party (indeed, Santana was still a member, while advocating political neutrality for FALINTIL). Meantime, many dissidents had been ill-treated.

'I defended the national unity policy,' the commander told me, 'I never understood communism—revolution, yes. Timor had to be for the Timorese, but I feared the radical policies FRETILIN adopted.'

He gave some examples of 'the many crimes committed in our support bases'. First was the detention and torture of founding FRETILIN president Xavier do Amaral on the grounds of being a 'feudal reactionary'. Afonso Savio, secretary of FRETILIN in the Lospalos region, was 'an ardent patriot accused of being Xavier's collaborator' who he said was beaten up and tortured, as was José Maria Andrade, who was branded with hot irons (a similar treatment afforded Do Amaral) and a man called Dos Santos, who the commander described as 'anti-communist but a passionate nationalist'.

The next morning was to be another 3 am start in order to arrive at the jungle location before daylight. Whereas the guerrillas had been dressed in jeans and T-shirts the previous day, they were all wearing variations of uniform for this excursion and were well-armed, with rifles, knives and grenades. The night was as moonless as the previous, and we were to move in single file, soundlessly and rapidly. They were accustomed to marching by night and had the reflexes and keen eyesight of experienced bushmen. And while their bodies might still be riddled with bullets, their hardiness and knowledge of the terrain was reflected in their swift progress along our invisible path. Konis marched in front of me, with several bodyguards behind and in front. Somehow I maintained the pace but stumbled on several occasions, sounding like an elephant crashing around in the undergrowth. I was comforted when the commander later stumbled and fell noisily himself.

Long after we had left the safe house we came to a village, where he whispered to me that extreme care should be taken because we were passing an SGI barracks, base of the military intelligence police. We walked right by it, as all the dogs in the village barked in chorus. Our shadowy file was without doubt visible to anyone who drew a curtain, but the night belonged to the guerrillas by unspoken agreement. They would not be challenged. The villagers no doubt drew secret comfort from their passing presence.

After an hour or so we reached a coffee plantation.

We were fairly high in the mountains and it was cold and damp. The terrain was heavily wooded and uneven, slowing progress, but eventually we found a place to huddle in total silence, until the sun came up. Its first rays were welcome as our bodies began to absorb some warmth.

We discussed how we would do the photo session. Santana had rustled up a video camera left by some previous journalist. I had never used one, but we had practised earlier in the safe house. He had a good mastery of the camera, and could set it up for me. There was no tripod, so we decided to balance it on a rock and sit the commander before it, filming from one unadventurous position to ensure results, though I would also film a scene of them all filing through the jungle, to provide a visual context. Then there would be a still photo session.

As we were talking I was amazed to see a group of women walking towards us through the plantation. They bore trays with steaming pots of coffee and freshly baked bread rolls. They served us attentively and we stretched out in a grassy clearing for an unforgettable meal, a species of 'Lunch on the Grass, with Guerrillas', while the bodyguards formed look-outs at the perimeter. I became aware that the plantation was perched on a hillside above a main road, and that everyday traffic, probably including Indonesian military vehicles, was roaring along below us.

Suddenly our security was breached, due to the inattention of the guards. A bare-torsoed Timorese man strode into view, a large machete swinging in his hand. He paused, his eyes registering fear as he realised there was a substantial group of uniformed, armed men before him, not to mention a middle-aged white lady. One of the guards came and took him by one arm, sitting him down gently. He presented a serious danger, not because he might raise the alarm immediately—he was outnumbered—but because he might talk later. Konis then moved over and sat down with him. He took his hand in his and spoke to him in a soft, earnest voice. Later I was given the gist of the conversation. 'Do you know who we are?' he asked, explaining that they were guerrillas from FALINTIL, who were fighting for everyone's independence, to drive out the occupiers. It seemed the man owned some of the coffee trees here, and had innocently walked up to harvest some beans. He was sure he must be a patriot, the commander continued, and he, Konis Santana, knew that he could count on his support. As a reward for his silence he gave him a pistol and asked him to join their force in the mountains as soon as he could. Tranquillised, the man walked slowly away.

We began the television interview, then the photographic work. Comandante Santana was wearing a military beret with black and green camouflage fatigues. We knew each other well now so he spoke without nervousness, cocking his head to one side in that characteristic way, giving off a handsome image with a touch of Che Guevara about it, which is still engraved in my mind. He spoke of the guerrilla's life as an honourable one, and their struggle as giving continuity to that of compatriots who had fallen before them.

He described the balance of forces on the ground, listing the Indonesian battalions active in East Timor, against Jakarta's denials that a war was in progress. He ranged over political questions, dealing authoritatively with a recent UN-brokered accord made in Geneva between Indonesia and Portugal, in consultation with Timorese diplomats. He spoke sadly of the difficulties of fighting without material support and the fact that resistance representatives abroad had delivered only US$4,500 of the funds collected in Portugal since 1991. He made a direct appeal to refugees abroad to give alternative backing:

> I have made a new appeal to the Timorese community abroad to contribute, but it hurts me. We all feel hurt by this …

> FALINTIL the liberation army fights for *all* Timorese of whatever political party. I appeal to them to support the guerrilla movement. If each month every Timorese sacrificed a trip to the cinema, or to the football, or a can of beer and sent the money to us, we could have $1,000 a month, which would serve … I appeal to the conscience of the Timorese abroad.[16]

Later that day I took my leave of Santana and his fellow fighters in a round of embraces, assuring them I would do my best to return soon. I looked for some paper for him to write on, to record our meeting, but I had used it all. My eyes lit on the formidable Anna Forbes. He adorned the reverse title page of her *Unbeaten Tracks in Islands of the Far East* with a fulsome text recording our encounter:

> I register in this space an event of transcendental importance which will never be forgotten by those who today fight for peace, liberty, justice and independence! The Maubere People will register this fact, which moves and honours us, in the pages of their history!
>
> On the eve of the glorious day of 20 August, the nineteenth anniversary of the founding of FALINTIL, I greet you in the name of all the guerrillas, wishing you the best in your task of informing and sensitising [the world] on behalf of the Maubere People, in defence of the truth!
>
> With the embrace of a friend,
>
> Nino Konis Santana

I was later escorted to the church of Lete-foho, where Father Soares awaited me. That evening he introduced one of his parishioners. The man had just survived a dreadful session of interrogation under torture in Dili. He wanted to give testimony for publication, so we agreed on a pseudonym that would protect him (‘*Makikit*’, meaning ‘eagle’), and I took a detailed account of his ordeal.

Next morning the priest organised a ride to Dili for me, sitting in a huge yellow lorry between two burly coffee workers, with no attempt at disguise. It was downhill all the way. It had taken seven difficult weeks to reach here, but we trundled down that mountain in the soft morning light in a joyful instant. They dropped me at the Dili bus station, a little out of town, where I boarded a bus to Kupang as it prepared to depart.

8
Exit

Kupang–Singapore, 14–19 August 1994

I broke my rule against air travel in order to travel on as rapidly as possible. I took a plane from Kupang to Jakarta, bearing my precious videotapes, photos and notes, and contacted F.F. on arrival. He had no knowledge of my whereabouts since the abortive conversation with Tommy in Suai, and he was delighted with news of the success. I still had to get over the border satisfactorily, and we made arrangements for an *estafeta* to carry key press material to Singapore, as a safeguard in case I was arrested on exit. The money F.F. was holding for me was just sufficient for a plane to Batam and then a hydrofoil on to the island republic.

But first, leavetaking. The Timorese underground in Jakarta organised a small party. We went to the darkened Anco park, emptied of daytime crowds, and drank Tiger beer accompanied by potato crisps. I met Virgílio Guterres, an activist and journalist who had recently completed a prison term, and two teenaged women who were officially students but also dedicated couriers for the resistance. They carried documents and correspondence regularly by plane and boat between Jakarta and Dili, risking the torture chamber if caught. They were all so admirable, and I was conscious that my success had been theirs. I was moved by this farewell gesture. As we chatted and drank, a rat jumped over our feet, in a final Indonesian march-past.

Xanana had replied to my interview questions, but F.F. was upset because instead of returning the answers by the same couriers with whom the questions had entered Cipinang prison, he had used the conventional network, deemed unreliable. It meant that people in an organisation considered infiltrated by INTEL knew of my presence in Indonesia. Until that time the information had been restricted to a small group whose allegiance was beyond question. Nevertheless the reply had come, and hopefully I would be over the border soon. I later received a copy of the Xanana text from a foreign activist in the Darwin wing of the network, saying how surprised she was to hear I was in Indonesia, but was too annoyed to reply.

F.F. took delivery of the press material to be carried out separately by a Timorese courier and I flew on to Batam. From there I rang the *Age* newspaper in Melbourne, and spoke to Russ Skelton, by chance an old university friend. Speaking carefully, I conveyed that I had a major story, and he asked me to call again when I arrived in Singapore.

I landed at Singapore wharf late the next day with less than 20 dollars in my pocket, wearing the ragged remains of the clothes with which I had travelled two months before (some had been burnt in the Borneo Hostel fire and the most vermin-ridden had been thrown out). The budget was only fit for a flophouse that night, and I rang Russ first thing the next day, telling him of my meeting with Santana and the guerrillas, and the written interview with Xanana. He told me to check in to the Sheraton Towers, the most expensive hotel in Singapore, and put everything on the bill—and to start writing. The *Age* would fax the manager telling them to put the room and all expenses on the bill, and to issue me a cash payment for everyday needs. Its large, deep bed felt abnormally soft.

I had carried out my diaries, written from start to finish in a rough code omitting proper names and places, so was able to begin the articles. However, I needed the photographic material, as the paper was anxious to publish as soon as possible and was dependent on the arrival of the courier, whoever that would be. I rang F.F., who said to watch the boats from Batam. I promised to wait at the wharf to oversee his or her smooth entry past officialdom. Two days later the story was ready to go, but there were no photos, and no news of the *estafeta*—lost, arrested? I assured Russ the material would arrive soon but my confidence was waning.

In late afternoon there was a call from reception. There was someone to see me, they said. Descending, my foot sprang over the soft, white carpet before the reception desk. With a just-discernible sniff, the manager extended his arm dramatically in the direction of a wild-eyed boy with a shaved head and a piratical bandana round it. Fresh from the jungle. I shuffled him quickly to a corner to speak, but we seemed to lack a word of any language in common, except 'Senhora', the Portuguese form of address. He did understand a smidgeon of that language when I persevered, because the Tetum spoken in Dili is full of Portuguese words. Under the curious eyes of the stiff-backed, perfectly groomed Sheraton staff, I bundled him rapidly into the lift and up to the room. He had all my video tapes and film. Somehow he had negotiated his way through Singaporean customs and immigration and found the hotel, but he was little more than a child, overwhelmed by the dangerous mission entrusted to him, which he had performed to perfection. His name was Natalino Domingos, he was 16, and he'd never previously been out of East Timor. I telephoned F.F. and chewed him out. 'How could you endanger the life of such a child?' I asked. 'He's my little brother and he's the only person we could get a passport for,' he replied lamely.

The kid had my gratitude, and pity (not that he needed such a condescending emotion: he was proud of doing his revolutionary duty). Like me, he had arrived washed-out and exhausted, so I ordered a whacking great meal in the room, which was wheeled in on a silver service, and the two of us sat quietly demolishing it, bereft of words we could exchange.

When he was finished I tried to explain that unfortunately I couldn't organise a room for him here, but I would take him to a guest-house to sleep. With a gesture that indicated this wasn't a problem, he untied the bandana, lay down on the carpet, placed it over his face saying, 'Good night, *Senhora*,' and fell into a deep sleep.

When the *Age* story appeared, it occupied large columns of the paper. In the early edition the interview with Santana ran as the front-page lead, with a prominent colour photo of the commander, which continued in the body of the paper. There was a piece highlighting his angry attack on Australian policy and our lunch on the grass was the focus of a feature story with pictures. It assessed the conflict in East Timor and sent the message that they were still fighting, the war was not over, and they were just decent people seeking their legitimate right to live free of the cruelties of foreign occupation. Australian Olympic swimmer Susie O'Neill won a gold medal as the story was going to press, so it lost the lead in the second edition, but its impact remained strong.

The story was also run by the sister paper, the *Sydney Morning Herald*, while another version ran as front-page lead in Hong Kong's *Eastern Express*. It was also published by the Lisbon daily *O Público*, and broadcast on Radio Netherlands (important, because the station was widely monitored in Timor). The prison interview with Xanana, in which he cast doubt on Indonesia's alleged intention of a negotiated withdrawal from East Timor, ran prominently in the same media the next day.

F.F. was insistent that Natalino should turn round and come back as soon as possible. 'Make sure he returns immediately,' he stressed. After a quick sightseeing tour of Singapore I escorted him to the ferry, ensuring he had the ticket and ample money to reach Jakarta. He was carrying tapes from me for Xanana and Santana. His mood was sombre; he was dreading returning to the daily ordeal of hiding from INTEL and the constant dangers of life in the underground. He couldn't just be a boy. I sat with him briefly in the departure lounge and tried to transmit my solidarity and gratitude to him, but feared the site could be watched by Indonesian agents, so said goodbye and left. However, from the floor above there was a good view of the lounge, where I could watch until he had embarked safely. Boarding was announced over the loudspeakers and passengers gathered their luggage and began filing towards the gate. All, that is, except Natalino. A last call was made, but still he sat there, a small lonely figure to make one's heart bleed. Perhaps he would turn and run. Finally, just as the boat was due to cast off, he stood and walked slowly on board.

My amulet in my pocket, I flew back to Australia the next day to plan my return visit to Santana.

Book II

Capture

9
The Return

Heading for Sydney, I hoped to trade on the success of the newspaper stories to obtain an advance for a television program about the guerrillas.

I had recently directed my first full-length documentary, *The Pandora Trail*, a story of prostitution rackets in the European Union, where local and Third World women were being bought and sold like cattle. Also filmed undercover, it had been screened in Austria, Holland and Portugal to healthy ratings, so my credentials were reasonable.

I did the rounds of the BBC, CNN and ITN offices in Sydney without success, drafting budgets and seeking funds from bodies like the government-backed Film Finance Corporation. The same dilemma that had presented four months earlier was evident: that asking for money represented a potential breach of security. I stressed to all people approached that the project must be treated in confidentiality, but they had no concept of the dangers a leak of information would represent for those of us working in the field. I walked into one office to see the project outline I had written, with the word 'CONFIDENTIAL' writ large on it, thrown carelessly open across somebody's desk. Worse, it had been given to an ill-informed and chattering member of a Timor solidarity group for comment. I was painfully aware that the same underground network of Timorese that F.F. believed to be corrupt had connections with the community in Sydney, although most members were honest refugees unaware of the rottenness within.

I made a side trip to Melbourne and had a closed meeting with members of the Timorese community there, describing the guerrillas' needy situation, and playing the tape in which Konis Santana asked them to make small, regular sacrifices so that he could count on their help. Most were shocked and shamefaced at his words, and immediately resolved to rectify the situation. But there was a small minority I judged to be unhappy about this material being aired, who would not welcome a return visit to the commander.

Dateline, the flagship current affairs of Australia's multicultural SBS channel, proved interested in the new venture. Its executive producer was Greg Wilesmith, who agreed to underwrite the project. During my previous passage through Hong Kong seeking a camera operator, I had met Dutchwoman Irene Slegt at the Foreign Correspondents' Club. She had her own camera and had been freelancing around Asia for some time. She had experience in difficult situations, having been in Tiananmen Square during the repression of the democracy movement, as well as brushing with the Chinese secret police while working on stories about Tibet.

She had been keen to accompany me to East Timor on the first visit, even after ITN had laughed me out of their office, but the only finance available was from a Portuguese channel, which failed to transfer her agreed fee from Lisbon before the set departure date.

I contacted her again to describe SBS's offer, and she agreed to do the camera work. I was determined to learn from the last trip, so planned to hire a production assistant to fly into Bali ahead of us and rent a villa in the Kuta Beach district, normally thronged by Australian backpackers. I would then cross the border again by ferry, and catch a plane to Bali, all within the one day, to exclude the need to ever book into a hotel. No more dramas over passports.

Malla Nunn was an offbeat but efficient Swazilander

fresh out of film school who had been recommended as production assistant. She jumped at the offer, so planning took on its own momentum. When the money came in, there was a bank account to open, which we did at ANZ Bank in Martin Place, and air tickets to be booked. Malla's partner was Mark Lazarus, an American filmmaker also just starting out, and they invited me to move into their chaotic filmie pad in Bondi, a suburb where a lot of the Sydney film crowd lived. It was my first substantial period back in Australia since moving to Portugal in 1978, and I enjoyed it greatly. Bondi beach was a delight first thing in the morning, and the horrors of Labuanbajo's rats seemed old history in this amenable setting. I was happy and confident at the prospect of returning to visit Santana in comparative style: many of the previous problems had arisen through sheer lack of money.

I had sent a bundle of cuttings of my stories to F.F. and he was pleased with the result. The possibility of publishing under a pseudonym to make return less risky had been discussed, but it seemed self-defeating. The Timorese were keen to demonstrate that a banned person had broken the blockade, and I also wished to have it on record. 'Their bureaucracy is very clumsy,' F.F. observed, 'You can get away with doing it a second time. They wouldn't believe you'd try it again.' I agreed.

The plot of the proposed television documentary was to run like a road movie. The material we were dealing with was naturally dramatic—simply filming the journey to Santana's hideout and giving a thorough account of the guerrilla life when we got there would provide riveting viewing, if the first journey was anything to go on. Although we would establish base in Bali, the journey would be filmed from Jakarta eastward, using a description of the capital to set the background to the Suharto dictatorship. Partly because I had responsibility for someone other than myself, and partly because the venture would be hard enough anyway, I had taken the mental decision not to seek to film a military clash—the most I conceived of filming in this direction would be to march with and show a routine patrol of the FALINTIL guerrillas. The documentary would concentrate on re-interviewing Santana and showing the day-to-day life of the fighters.

One day there was an unexpected and alarming call from F.F. His people in Lisbon had sent him an article that had all the hallmarks of having been planted to discredit my work, and which could endanger the second expedition. The conservative daily *Diário de Notícias* had published a report by diplomatic correspondent Carlos Albino quoting Timorese leadership sources in Lisbon as saying I had gone to the mountains without authorisation from the resistance and also breached security in an interview, endangering the subject. How I could possibly have arrived at Santana's hideout without his agreement or the assistance of the dozens of Timorese resistance operatives who had ensured the success of the trip was a mystery. The claim that an interviewee had been endangered by the story was presumably a reference to Makikit, the torture victim, but the conditions had been thoroughly discussed and agreed with him, and his identity and whereabouts disguised accordingly. There had been no repercussions. Albino had made no attempt to seek comment from me. The article smelt of a manoeuvre to counteract my snapshot of the guerrillas, showing them fighting on courageously but feeling let down by their representatives abroad. It was the first of a series of problems that were to bedevil the return trip.

F.F. had asked me to write a new letter to Santana and other commanders seeking formal permission for the television report. He had already sent copies of my articles to them. 'They'd be crazy not to agree after seeing these,' he asserted. In the letter to Santana I asked if he could give a signed credential to any courier he sent as a security guarantee for us (while realising he might be reluctant to do this, because it could equally compromise the messenger and even set a trail to the commander himself).

After a solid briefing for Malla in which I tried to transmit the potential perils of the venture and the need for extreme discretion, she flew off to Bali to set up our household. A few days later she rang to say that she had rented a villa off Legian Road, the main tourist drag, conveniently screened from the street and run by some young Balinese men who seemed fairly laid-back. I then caught a plane to Malaysia, having discovered there was a ferry similar to the Singapore one plying between Kuala Lumpur and the Sumatran port of Medan. I re-entered the country without a hitch and caught a domestic flight from Medan to Denpasar, where she met me. We then called Irene to tell her it was OK to travel in. By now it was November 1994, and within a week the three of us were assembled in Bali ready to start work.

Like Benidorm in Spain, Bali's Kuta Beach was the sort of place discerning travellers avoided. Just as English tourists had denuded Benidorm of all its Spanish qualities, creating a bizarre piece of Little England replete with bangers and mash, Australians had turned this piece of Bali into a strip of characterless bars, and encouraged its residents to become a race of touts and sharpsters. Cheap Lycra sarongs and tasteless souvenirs had replaced the traditional arts of what was formerly a courtly Hindu society. After the terrorist bombing of 2002, Australians developed a more thoughtful relationship with the island and its people, but in the meantime Kuta Beach was a hedonistic, commercialised tourist centre that served our purposes well—nobody thought to question the renting of a villa by three foreign women. It was to serve as our safe house for the duration of the project. Both Irene and I had an inordinate amount of luggage and equipment, which we needed to pare down before travel (I was carrying painkillers, toothache remedies, a still camera and a range of first aid materials for Santana, as well as my own gear). We would leave the excess in the house with Malla and sort it out on return.

F.F. had promised to come to Bali soon to meet the crew and map out our program. During a pre-breakfast training jog I saw him walking into view, with another Timorese I hadn't met before. I showed them to the villa, and we all sat down to talk. He introduced his companion as José Reis, younger brother of Vicente Reis, a FRETILIN founder whose reputation almost equalled that of Nicolau Lobato. Vicente was from a noble family in the hamlet of Bucoli, near Baucau, and was one of a group of radical students who had studied in Portugal and fallen under the influence of Marxist-Leninist ideas. Yet he had never been connected with fanaticism, nor with the ill-treatment of alleged dissidents described by Santana. On the contrary, there were many stories of his role as a gentle teacher behind guerrilla lines, and he had died a lingering death from untreated wounds sometime around the period Lobato was killed. Such was his legend that in a later period, well after the Indonesian army's withdrawal from East Timor, an animist cult known as The Sacred Family preached that Vicente and other guerrilla heroes would rise from the dead and emerge from the jungle. It was able to assemble thousands of followers to await his resurrection at a given spot. José must have been much younger than him, because when I met him in Bali he looked the same age as Vicente was when I first knew him in the 1970s. The resemblance showed in his physical appearance, style and intelligence.

F.F. explained that José was working as a civil servant in Indonesia's foreign ministry, and had seen a memo concerning my published stories from the Santana visit. 'The official line is that they are all fabricated because you were a banned person who couldn't possibly enter Indonesia,' he chuckled.

There were hopes on all sides that we would avoid the long waiting period that had marred the first trip and F.F. seemed to have things in hand. The pair returned to Jakarta and promised to call soon.

Some days later they rang to say that a courier had appeared who claimed to be from Santana. He did not carry a written credential, but this was not necessarily meaningful. F.F. and Tommy had decided to interview him separately to test his story. If he passed their scrutiny he would then be presented to us to discuss details of the journey.

We locked the house and headed off to Jakarta, booking initially into the Borneo Hostel and then an even cheaper establishment in Jalan Jaksa. Irene and I began working from the storyboard I had constructed, setting out the general history of the East Timorese struggle and the role of the underground in Jakarta. We filmed an interview with F.F. on the waterfront at Anco Park, and shots of Tommy monitoring the BBC news and the daily papers, which were reflecting the ferment underway in the ranks of Suharto's ruling elite. In the wake of the Santa Cruz massacre Ali Alatas had described the East Timor problem as being like 'a pebble in a shoe—if it hurts, get rid of it', indicating that divisions were appearing among the Indonesian elite.[17]

Jakarta was to host a meeting of APEC, the Asia-Pacific Economic Cooperation forum, and the East Timorese had decided to use the presence of world leaders in Jakarta, including the American president, to highlight their cause. Students began jumping the fences of foreign embassies and demanding political asylum. Most were survivors of the Santa Cruz massacre who were being hunted by INTEL. Indonesian security authorities had consequently upgraded their vigilance in East Timor, creating a tense atmosphere in both Dili and Baucau, and it also affected Jakarta, creating unwanted extra difficulties for our work. The press there was focused on a large group of students who had scaled the wall of the American embassy and were holed up inside. The building was surrounded by BRIMOB, the anti-riot police. Irene and I would have liked to cover this event, at least to film for inclusion in the documentary, but decided not to risk sacrificing our larger project. We reluctantly satisfied ourselves with some quick drive-pasts to peep at what was happening.

Having laid the foundations for the documentary, we were ready to begin the long journey east.

We were to meet F.F. and Tommy at the Dunkin' Donuts shop in a mall near the Indonesia Hotel. There they would present the courier, who had passed the preliminary tests. We took a round-about route to ensure we weren't being followed. I had earlier asked F.F. to speak with Irene in English as much as possible, as I found it psychologically wearing to translate from Portuguese to English at the same time as I was trying to conduct a complicated conversation.

My first impressions of the man who claimed to be an envoy from the guerrillas were positive. He was a large, strong-looking lad with tribal tattoos on his arms and a ready smile. He looked like a mountain person. We had no common language, so F.F. translated from Tetum. I reminded him that it would be important when we got to the mountains to be accompanied always by an English- or Portuguese-speaker, which he agreed with. Having no common spoken language could prove disastrous in an emergency.

Despite my request, most of our conversation in Dunkin' Donuts ended up being conducted between F.F. and me in Portuguese, with him translating from the envoy's Tetum to Portuguese, which I would then translate to Irene in English where possible. We didn't know his name or ask it, judging it to be an unnecessary risk for him. I called him 'A'.

Using this system of translation, I explained to 'A' just

exactly what we wanted to do, and what our respective roles were. I wished to return to Santana to conduct a new interview, and to film our journey along the way, I told him, and Irene was there as camera operator.

We discussed the logistics of the journey and he seemed to understand what was needed. At one point, however, he noted that the date of 7 December was approaching, the 19th anniversary of the Indonesian invasion of East Timor. He suggested that, if we liked, the guerrillas could stage an attack for us.

I didn't dignify this proposal with a response: I wasn't in the business of theatre or cheap tricks. No self-respecting journalist would enter into such a pact, although a few do from time to time.

The outcome of the meeting was acceptance by all sides to press ahead with the project, accepting 'A' as the envoy. He would travel east immediately to prepare the ground and we would follow, filming the route as we went.

We returned to Bali by bus and boat and had a brief glimpse of 'A' on the deck of the ferry between Java and Lombok, but none of us registered recognition. We planned to see him again in West Timor.

Travel would be faster and easier on this occasion. Leaving Malla as our anchorperson in Bali, Irene and I were to catch a flight from Denpasar to Maumere in Flores. From there we would travel to Larantuka, on the eastern tip of the same island, where I was anxious to get some general shots of the Florinese in their cultural setting, and record vestiges of Portugal's previous colonial presence.

The filming went well. By the time we left Bali we already had quite a lot of material in the can—we had captured some of the eerie, dictatorial aspects of the Suharto dictatorship as seen from Jakarta—the omnipresent police, the moustachioed INTEL agents (my 'Tonton Macoutes') peering out from street corners—and we had captured the atmosphere of the Third World rattletrap bus that jolted us across Java to a cacophony of latest Indonesian hits and an occasional kung fu video. Irene filmed the landing of our light plane with great professionalism, capturing its wheels hitting the ground through the window, while remaining firm on her feet. On arrival we hired a *bemo* to Larantuka.

Larantuka had always had a certain magic about it. The Portuguese colonisation of Timor had begun from here in the early 16th century. They had first set foot on Timor's north coast around 1512, but didn't settle until much later. Instead, they built a fort at nearby Solor Island and Dominican priests worked from there and Larantuka. The Portuguese remained on the island until Governor Lopes da Lima sold it to the Dutch in the mid-18th century. According to C.R. Boxer, the great scholar of colonial Asia, the Dutch and Portuguese attempted to settle their borders in 1850. Although he had no authority to do so, Governor Lopes de Lima traded Portugal's settlements on Flores and Solor to the Dutch in exchange for Portugal's takeover of Maubara (then a Dutch enclave in East Timor) and 200,000 florins. The Portuguese government repudiated the deal and he was recalled home in disgrace—but as it never did find the money to repay the sum paid by the Dutch, Flores became an irretrievable piece of the Dutch colonial empire.

I knew from the work of Portuguese diplomat António Pinto da França that the Catholic church in Larantuka used a semi-secret liturgy in archaic Portuguese for certain ceremonies in the religious calendar, such as Easter.

Pinto da França had been Portuguese ambassador to Indonesia in the early 1960s and was a friend of President Sukarno. They had struck up a friendship after Sukarno married his second wife Dewi, a beautiful Japanese woman who was considerably younger than him. Sukarno was concerned to keep her amused and, as Ambassador Pinto da França's wife was her age, he invited the couple to socialise with them regularly. I came to know the ambassador in Angola in the 1980s when he was based there and working on his book *Portuguese Influence in Southeast Asia*, which was published by the Gulbenkian Foundation. We talked about East Timor's occupation by Indonesia, then of great concern to Lisbon, but he also liked to spin colourful yarns of Sukarno's Indonesia.

The liveliest and most vivid accounts of Larantuka, however, come from Boxer, who wrote:

> It was sandalwood that attracted the Portuguese to Timor about the same time as they reached the Spice Islands, soon after Albuquerque's conquest of Malacca in 1511. Their first recorded settlement in the Lesser Sunda group dates from 1566, when some Dominican missionary friars built a stone fort on the island of Solor in order to afford protection to the converts they had recently made among the natives of the Flores and Solor groups. Around this fort there grew up a settlement populated by the offspring of Portuguese soldiers, sailors and traders from Malacca and Macao, who intermarried with the local women. This mixed race, and the natives who were connected with them, were later called the Topasses ... and similar communities made their appearance in due course in the eastern half of Flores and Timor ...
>
> The Dutch attacked and took the fort on Solor in April 1613, and the Portuguese then shifted their base to Larantuka on the eastern tip of Flores, where they founded a settlement that gave the Dutch constant trouble ...
>
> The Topasses—or *Larantuqueiros* as they were also called from their new base—received a fresh injection of European blood when the Dutch commander of Solor Jan de Hornay, deserted to Larantuka in 1629, turned Roman Catholic and married a Timorese slave girl by whom he had two sons. This was the origin of the family of De Hornay or De Ornay, who were later transported to Timor and provided some of the most powerful chieftans on that island, alternatively champions and enemies of Portuguese rule ...
>
> Larantuka remained the centre of Portuguese influence in the Lesser Sunda islands throughout the 17th century and

> although the Dutch successively drove the Portuguese from all other settlements between the Moluccas and Malabar they never succeeded in stamping out this particular hornets'-nest.
>
> ... During the second half of the seventeenth century, the viceroys at Goa made sporadic attempts to enforce their nominal authority over Solor and Timor by appointing governors in the name of the Crown, but the Dominican friars combined with the Hornays and Costas to expel these unwanted intruders. The viceroys constantly complained of the turbulence, intractability and even the immorality of the Dominican missionaries in Timor, whom they more than once thought of replacing by Jesuits.[18]

According to Boxer, the viceroy later complained of the Dominicans that their fruit was 'not so much that which they gathered in the vineyard of the Lord, as that which they begat in the freedom and licentiousness in which they lived'. In their defence, he wrote, one Dominican vicar-general had complained that the local women were 'exceedingly lascivious' and forced their way into the houses of the younger clergy, 'leaving them with no option but flight from their own homes'.[19]

Irene and I did find some symbols of the Portuguese connection, but were limited in what we could film without arousing suspicion. There was a church with a contemporary mural depicting Portuguese sailing ships, but our request to film it was met with hostility by its nuns. Their response may have come from fear. It was hard to read below the surface, but there were evident tensions in the air—most Florinese must have known that only a short distance to their south a war was continuing in Timor. I had even heard rumours that some survivors of the massacre were being hidden here. Showing interest in anything Portuguese could invite trouble, by suggesting disloyalty to the Indonesian army.

So we satisfied ourselves with discreet filming of the local graveyard, where tombstones bore the symbol of Santa

Cruz, borne by Portugal's 16th-century navigators, and featured names such as 'Da Silva', 'Da Costa', 'Hornay', 'Pedro', 'Lorenzo' and 'Francisco'.

From Larantuka I telephoned F.F. with a progress report. He told me that one of his supporters had infiltrated the distrusted Dili-based network and monitored messages between it and Jaime[20], one of the resistance representatives abroad, which indicated that they knew of our journey. 'Take care,' he told me, 'Jaime has told them in Dili that you're an agent of BAIS.' This was disconcerting news, BAIS being the feared Armed Forces Strategic Intelligence Unit (*Badan Inteligen Strategis*) and uninformed resistance supporters would certainly treat any foreigner linked to it with hostility. Utmost caution was needed in the period ahead.

That evening we sailed on the Larantuka-Kupang ferry. It was an uneventful trip except for the unwelcome attention of a talkative English-speaking man from Flores. He struck up a conversation in a casual way, asking what we did and who we were. Irene told him she was a consultant on environmental issues, while I brought Jane Carlton back from the dead. His questions became so insistent that we had to make a concerted effort to indicate politely but firmly that we were tired of talking. He had asked where we would stay in Kupang, and I had given him the name of the *losmen* I had chosen, in order to appear open and honest. It was by now the early hours of the morning.

The boat progressed steadily across the Savu Sea. Most passengers were sleeping on the darkened lower deck, with the only sound being of waves breaking on the ship's bow. After our rebuff the questioner sank back on his rattan mat, his face disappearing in the dark. Then he began to sing 'Irene Goodnight', as if in ironic tribute to Irene. Years later I remember his unaccompanied voice floating through the warm tropical air with the words of Huddy Ledbetter.

It had always been one of my favourite blues songs, but I felt compelled to search it out again. It tells of the singer's doomed courtship of a young girl whose parents discover his attempted seduction and force her to reject him. Sad and fatalistic, in the original version the singer warns: 'If Irene turns her back on me, I'm going to take morphine and die.' Later, it seemed like an anthem for our ill-fated expedition.

10
Doubts and Fears

I was anxious before landing in Kupang. The backlash from the APEC demonstrations was continuing, with arrests and heightened security. It was a really unlucky coincidence for us, but there was nothing to be done. Fortunately there was only a visual check of incoming passengers on this occasion, no demand for documents or bag search.

The wharf was some distance from town, and we caught a crowded *bemo*. As we travelled along the beach road to the outskirts of Kupang we came across an amazing sight. The frigate *Johannes*, Margaret Thatcher's gift to the Indonesian military, was moored right in front of us.[21] The tide was low and its bow loomed up as though the whole vessel was teetering on the beach before us. It was perfect proof that British military hardware was being used in the Timorese theatre of war. The streets were full of Battalion 743 soldiers enjoying their last leave before boarding to head east. I so wanted to photograph it, but there were too many eyes watching. We couldn't throw away the big story we were pursuing for a lesser one. Besides, for a writer the eye is a camera. It was more frustrating for Irene because she was working entirely in a visual medium. I saw her reach for the video camera but whispered to her to please not do it. Such a pity.

When we arrived at the *losmen*, I was startled to see our questioner from Flores standing outside, with a man on a motorbike who appeared to be a local official. He turned his face from view as we approached. Returning to the hotel later in the day, after lunch in town and purchase of some needed supplies, I caught a tall man exiting from my room. He didn't appear to be a member of staff. Alarm bells were ringing, but I was determined to keep cool, remembering all the reverses of the August venture. From 1975 I had learnt that there was a certain serendipity about working in Timor. Just when things looked totally hopeless the situation could change completely. Sometimes one had to shut one's eyes and hope for the best—the success of any dangerous assignment depends to an extent on luck as well as on planning and determination.

I kept these problems mainly to myself in the belief that I could resolve them. Irene seemed a little anxious, but the situation was new to her and she still seemed to believe that my constant suspicions and insistence on elaborate security were just paranoia, that I imagined things.

The next step was to catch a bus to Atambua where we would meet up with 'A' and hopefully be taken straight towards our target. We were making good time, and if things didn't fall apart, we should have a substantial amount of time to film and march with the guerrilla fighters.

My fear that we had been under surveillance in Kupang meant our departure from the city needed to be well-planned, and we took detailed precautions against being followed. We left very early, and changed buses often. Things proceeded normally, and the two of us travelled calmly and quietly together throughout the day. We seemed to have quit the West Timorese capital without a hitch. At one point, near the town of Kefamenanu, a rather large Indonesian with a floppy tennis hat sitting directly behind me caught my eye, but I had no reason to suspect him—he just looked a bit different.

By evening we had booked into a *losmen* in Atambua. I rang F.F. to report on our whereabouts and he passed on another chilling warning. 'Jaime has told them in Dili not only that you are working for Indonesian intelligence, but that your mission is to destroy the CNRM [*Conselho Nacional da Resistência Maubere*—National Council of Maubere Resistance, the principal resistance coordinating body], and you must be stopped at any cost,' he said. Because our journey had been planned completely independently of the Dili organisation, there was no reason it shouldn't succeed if we were careful, although this was a problem we did not need. I fretted over it, but still believed we would reach the guerrillas.

We seemed set for a long wait for our guides. After two days in Atambua, there was no sign of 'A', and I called Jakarta again to find out what the problem was. 'Hold tight, they're coming,' Zely advised.

Indeed they were. Soon after I called, a jeep with East Timor numberplates sped ostentatiously into the yard of the *losmen*, with 'A' and two other young men tumbling out. They were visible to all. The pair with him were introduced as Talofo and Julião, which I assumed to be *noms de guerre*. The latter indicated he had been assigned to the project for his English-language skills, yet he could barely form a sentence in English: we would be reduced to communicating in sign-language with the three of them. We grabbed our gear, checked out of the hotel and departed. I discovered that if I spoke slowly with 'A' in Portuguese he could understand a bit. For the rest it was either Indonesian or Tetum, and I cursed my laziness in depending on Portuguese, which so few young people spoke now, instead of making the effort to master Tetum.

I wore a baggy Rastafarian-style peaked cap that I could pull down over my forehead and a Cambodian scarf (*krama*)—fondly known among journalists as a 'sweat rag'—to cover the rest of my face. Both of us had black gloves to cover our white hands. Nevertheless, we were two white women travelling with a group of young men with profiles fitting those of resistance supporters. I hoped we would not be stopped and questioned. We kept our heads down and faces away from the windows as much as possible. If we were stopped, the only course would be to keep cool and let the lads do most of the talking.

Things went well until we had almost reached Dili. 'A' managed to convey that there was an Indonesian road-block on the outskirts of the capital. He said they had a fishing boat on standby at Tibar, a few kilometres before it, and that they would transfer us to it, sail us down the coast beyond the roadblock, and then fetch us on the other side. The three of them then began arguing in Tetum, becoming quite agitated, and I soon noticed that we had passed the Tibar fishing beach.

It was dark by now, and without notice we swung around the last curve taking us into Dili, screeching to a halt at a substantial military checkpoint staffed by swaggering, uniformed Indonesian soldiers. 'A', who had been driving throughout, muttered something to the effect of 'Keep calm, we have this covered, it looks bad, but it's OK'. He got out and went to speak to some of them. The same soldiers came over to the vehicle and opened the back doors. One of them leant in and switched on a large torch, holding it first on Irene's face for some seconds, and then mine. We both stared ahead without flinching. They went off for another consultation, then 'A' called to Julião, who jumped out of the car and went over, offering a card to the group. After some more chat, the two of them returned. 'A' started the engine, and we were waved on. He explained to me that the card was a military pass they had managed to buy, or forge (it wasn't clear which) in Julião's name, sometime ago. They had left it behind as a guarantee. The story sounded strange, but then things did work in a strange way here.

We proceeded into the residential area of Dili. The car backed into a narrow street lined with terraces of concrete

Indonesian-style houses on each side. 'A' indicated we should keep quiet with our heads down. He backed into the driveway of one of the houses, parking the jeep so that it was right up to the door. We were then quickly hustled inside. As in Letefoho, it was the home of a normal Timorese family whose members worked for the Indonesian civil service by day and the resistance by night. Some of them spoke Portuguese. Irene and I were fed and shown our beds. We were asked to speak only in whispers—all the houses in the terrace were conjoined, and the walls did not go up to the ceiling. Almost all the neighbours just happened to be from the Indonesian military—we were in the heart of the monster.

I learnt from our hosts that we were to travel to the mountain range south of Baucau, not the Ermera district where I had interviewed Santana. This meant they were most likely taking us to Taur Matan Ruak, the chief-of-staff of FALINTIL. As we had weeks of reporting ahead of us, we would no doubt catch up with Comandante Santana further along the way. The mountains around Baucau had long been the effective heart of the military struggle, so should provide good material for our story.

'A' explained that they had to do some trial runs of the Dili-Baucau road to be satisfied we could travel along it in safety. It is less than 100 km long, but it curves around mountainsides high above the sea, and so takes more than two hours to negotiate. We would travel by night. There is a sheer cliff to the sea on one side for much of the way, with forested mountain rising up on the other. Because of these characteristics, it is not difficult for the military to control: just a few strategic observation points can guarantee knowledge of every passing vehicle.

For the next two days we huddled in the Dili house, speaking in whispers, as they drove the road repeatedly. They travelled it twice but were still not satisfied, so decided on a third run.

While we waited I gleaned interesting information from the householders about daily life in Indonesian-occupied Dili. I was moved to hear that during the 19 years since the 1975 invasion, the people of Dili congregated regularly in one another's homes in private prayer sessions imploring God to deliver them from the occupying power. They also prayed in the churches, but were subject to surveillance there. It was quite jarring to see the adults in the house leave for work each morning in the uniforms of the Indonesian civil service (which was organised on paramilitary lines). They straddled two disparate worlds. It was a tiny view of real life under the skin of the occupied city, one which definitively contradicted the claims of smug politicians abroad that the people of Timor had accepted Indonesian rule. I was acutely conscious that my own country, Australia, whose white majority had never been occupied by a foreign power, had conspired with the Suharto dictatorship for the annexation of East Timor. In practice it had sanctioned bombings, mass executions, arbitrary arrests and the routine use of torture on average citizens, who the dictatorship could accuse of the slightest infraction for simply being East Timorese.

The third trial proved successful, and 'A' announced that we would leave that evening.

11
Waiting for Death

Irene and I were steeled for the ordeal ahead when we departed from Dili that night. We knew how risky the project was, but held hopes of success, despite certain organisational failings which we had discussed together. Our inability to communicate easily with our Timorese companions worried us, and the scene at the roadblock had also left us uneasy. On the other hand we had many years of experience as journalists between us, including in extreme situations. We felt mentally prepared for one of the most dangerous assignments we would ever undertake, without illusions about the chances of failure. We just didn't count on it going as badly wrong as it did.

It was still light when we left, leaving Dili via a military post at the suburb of Becora, which gives access to the Baucau road. We kept our heads down and backs to the window, snatching a brief view of the cluster of Indonesian soldiers at the turn-off.

After nightfall we were swallowed into the endless black hole of the road stretching ahead, with an occasional silver glimpse of the ocean to our left. There was not a single vehicle on that road until we were about two-thirds of the distance to Baucau. Perhaps we were being observed by sentries in the mountain forest above, but it seemed as though all human activity on the half-island had ceased. Was it again a case of the Indonesian army leaving the night to the guerrillas?

When we were around the two-thirds mark, 'A' stopped the car, complaining of a malfunction. I groaned inwardly—

a breakdown was out of the question. Irene and I got out and hid beside it, away from the road. As he tinkered under the bonnet, another car pulled up, the only civilian vehicle we were to encounter on the coast road that night. The driver was Father Baltazar from the Salesian mission at Fatumaca, beyond Baucau, well-known as a logistical support base for the guerrillas. He spoke with our companions briefly, then got in his car and travelled on. Soon after, they decided the car was fixed and we also climbed in and resumed our journey. It seemed probable that this encounter was not a chance one, and that there had been no mechanical problem, but it was hard for an outsider to decipher the myriad codes and signals by which they operated. Quite simply, we were largely in their hands and there were certain things we had to take on trust, although we would never abdicate our right to determine our own safety in the ultimate instance. A balance had to be drawn between the two.

We were almost to Baucau when Irene told me a darkened car had pulled off the side of the road, turned on its lights, and was following behind us. I had been concentrating on keeping my head down out of view and nerves under control, so had not seen it. The voices of the Timorese rose in excited staccato exchanges and 'A' slammed his foot down on the accelerator. The car was a maroon four-wheel drive with smoked-glass windows, the type favoured by INTEL, and there was no doubt that it was now pursuing us. We reached Baucau, and a high-speed chase began through its back streets. 'A' decided he was going to lose the pursuer at any cost and started manoeuvring, twisting and turning through the streets at a frightening velocity. The maroon car disappeared temporarily from view. He approached a lone house by the roadside with a single bulb illuminating the verandah like a spotlight. '*Sai! Sai!*' he screamed, 'Get out! Get out!' They wanted to separate from us, so as not to be caught with journalists in the car. They would return. He didn't stop, trying to get us to jump from it while it was still moving. 'No!' I shouted in Portuguese, 'You must stop!' He slowed almost to a halt and we exited somehow, half-jumping, half-falling. I managed to grab only a small bag with my wallet and passport; Irene seized the bag with her video camera in the last seconds before the Timorese sped off.

We were on a low road leading out of Baucau. On a road above, voices could be heard, people running. Soldiers were stirring. We ran into the house. I had no idea why they had shoved us towards it, my only guess being that its occupants must be part of the Baucau underground, and that they were handing us on to them for protection. But all we saw was a household of terrified people. They were standing in a row, an old man and woman, and several young people. One was a girl in her late teens or early 20s, who spoke some Portuguese. She was screaming, 'Go away! We can't hide you! The military are already leaving the barracks!' Indeed, I could hear vehicles revving up. We brushed past and out the back door, searching for a hiding-place. We crouched in a goat pen, but they followed us, imploring us to leave. We realised that it would be dreadful to implicate them. 'Please, please,' I asked the girl, 'Could you just show us the road to the forest? We'll hide in the bush for the night. Just show us the road ...'

She and a brother grabbed our hands and led us some distance down a path before releasing us and running back to the house. I saw a figure in shadow ahead, the glow of a cigarette butt. I assumed they were handing us on to him, and walked in his direction, addressing him in Portuguese. I saw that at least he was Timorese, but I had misjudged the situation. Instead of responding to me, he turned and began to run up a hill, shouting to an unknown listener in Indonesian: '*Dua wanita! Dua wanita!*' ('Two women! Two women!') We began to run again, but I stumbled and fell, striking my knee painfully. Irene was slim and lithe and I was unfit and around 12 years older than her. 'Grab my hand,' she said, 'I'll help you along,' but we had no idea where we could go. We had lost control of our fate, and it would probably only be a matter of minutes before soldiers appeared. 'Irene, stop a moment,' I said, 'We need to think through what we're going to do. Let's sit here under this tree.' We lowered ourselves to the ground and fought to regain our breath. As we did, I saw that there was a deep monsoon drain below us, overgrown with brambles. I pointed it out to her. 'We've got to get in this drain and lie perfectly still, not moving a muscle, for hours,' I said. 'It's the only way to save our lives.'

We fell into it and lay down, and it was extremely uncomfortable. Fortunately it was dry, but it had largish rocks in it, which poked into my back. Irene has long legs, and, like me, she was on her back with her knees crooked. Our feet were almost meeting, with our heads up each end, but her legs were sticking above the line of the ditch and could possibly be seen. I whispered urgently for her to lower them, but she was having difficulty. Maybe there was no further room for her to move up, and I certainly couldn't move back. There was something alive in the ditch behind me, which moved occasionally. Whether it was a snake or a rat, I didn't know and I didn't care. I wasn't moving for an hour or so.

After we settled I whispered to her urgently: 'I'm so sorry, Irene, so sorry, I didn't mean to get you into this.'

The informer who had run up the hill knew exactly where he had last seen us, and soon there was a search under way. I calculated the time it started as about 8 pm. The longest night of my life began. We could hear motorbikes and cars cruising along the street, and men walking. They came very close to us. Then what appeared to be a spotlight illuminated everything above us—the brambles, the sky, the tree. It seemed to be focused exactly on our location. After some

As the Suharto dictatorship draws towards its final years, ever-watchful police control Jakarta streets. © *Jill Jolliffe*

Suharto the Great Reaper looms over a city square on a Maoist-style billboard, Jakarta 1994. © Jill Jolliffe

Legendary guerrilla leader David Alex (left) receives Timorese journalists at his eastern base. © Eduardo Belo

Above: Nino Konis Santana enjoys a joke with his men, Mirtutu, 1994.
© Jill Jolliffe

Right: FALINTIL guerrilla commander Nuno Konis Santana, Mirtutu, 1994. © Jill Jolliffe

Jill Jolliffe with guerrilla commander Nino Konis Santana, Mirtutu 1994.

Nino Konis Santana (left) and guerrillas during a rest break in an Ermera coffee plantation. © *Jill Jolliffe*

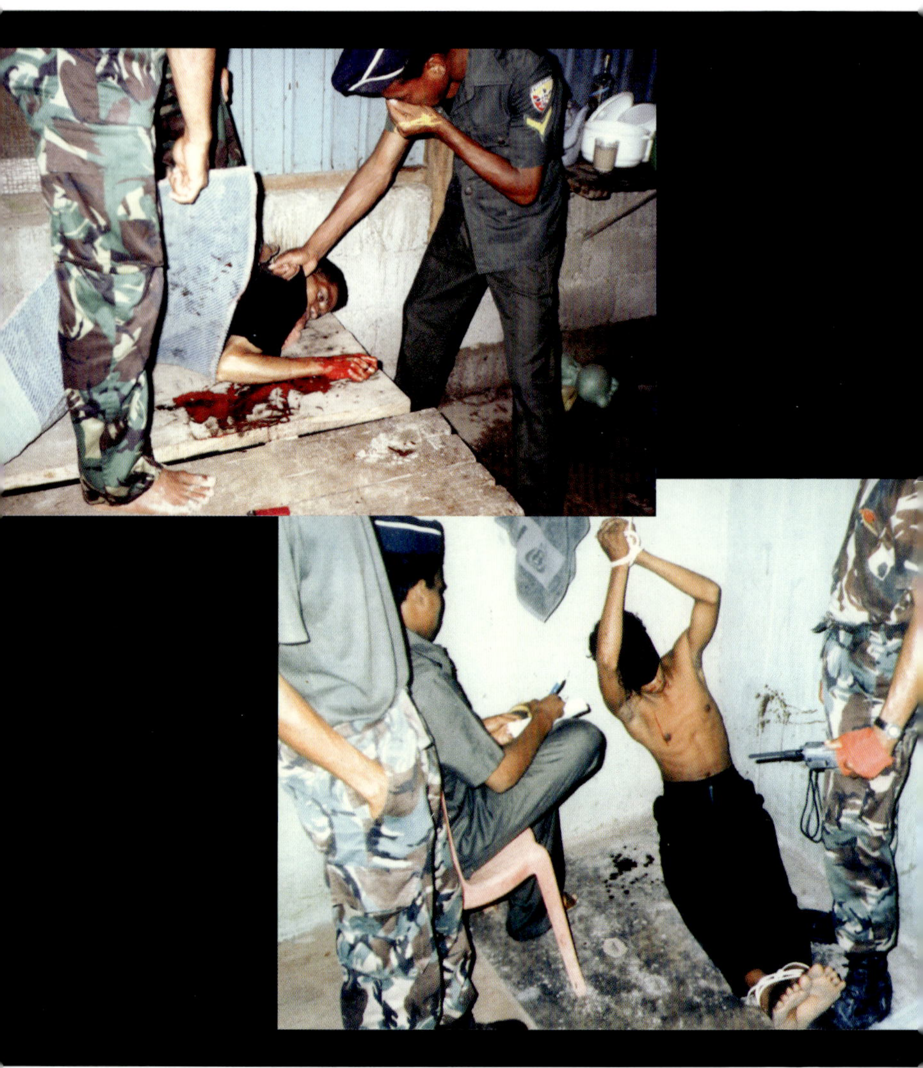

Top: Inside a Baucau torture chamber—a 1996 photo smuggled from East Timor shows the body of a youth captured on his way to Dili to welcome Bishop Carlos Belo on his return from Nobel Peace Prize ceremonies in Oslo.

Above: Timorese youth under torture during interrogation by an Indonesian officer, Baucau 1996.

time I realised it wasn't a conventional spotlight, but that the searchers had driven two cars up at different angles, crossing their headlights at the spot where we were. I hoped against hope that Irene's legs weren't showing. They walked alongside the drain, so close we could see their army boots and hear the crunch on gravel.

It was probably only a handful of men, but in our state of terror it seemed like the entire Indonesian army was scouring the bush for us. I was convinced it was only a matter of time before we were found and dragged out of there. Neither the Indonesian government nor the military recognised the independence of journalists. To them, the fact that we were travelling with resistance operatives—although there was no other way to reach the guerrillas—meant that we must be of them. They had killed six of us during the invasion in 1975. They called Timorese resistance supporters GPK, short for *gerombolan pengacau keamanan* or 'public security disturbers', a term to denote communists dating from Suharto's bloody purges of 1965, and to them we were one and the same. We would die that night, I thought. Being in the countryside, far from public scrutiny, they could do what they liked. The chance of escape was nil, the chance of survival slim. I feared above all that they might bayonet us in the ditch. Why they never looked down and saw us was a mystery, although much later one reason became apparent.

The manhunt continued thus for hours, as we lay perfectly immobile and mute. There were small lulls in their activity. During one, we realised dogs were involved. We could hear them near us, growling. Thinking it through, I reasoned that dogs have natural predators in the wild, some of which would be lying in ditches. There could be wild cats, lizards or snakes, so having sensed the presence of an animal, in this case human, was no guarantee it would go after it. But the growling could indicate our whereabouts to the watching soldiers. At one point during these hours of searching I thought I heard a drum or the sound of marching, until I realised it was my own heart, beating so abnormally loudly that I had mistaken it for something external to me. My heart might, indeed, give out before they found us.

Around 1 or 2 am they seemed to desist. Cars drove away, lights and torches disappeared, and voices faded. There was certainly no sign of anyone close any more. I didn't believe they had given up, but assumed they may have left sentries roughly encircling the position, and would resume the close search at daylight.

We took advantage of the change for a whispered conference. 'How do you intend to get out of this? Are we going to lie here all night?' Irene asked.

'It's obvious we're going to be caught, there's no escape,' I replied, 'but we musn't surrender at night, they can just kill us. If we wait until dawn, Timorese people will start circulating in the streets. That's a protection. We'll get out and try and find the local priest to accompany us to the police station.'

She agreed to this strategy but still held to another hope. 'Maybe "A" and the others got away and really will come back for us,' she said.

'I don't think so', I whispered, 'but I suppose it's possible.'

We settled in to wait for dawn. As we lay there facing what could be our last hours, we witnessed a strange phenomenon. Stars began falling from the sky in a spectacular display of galactic fireworks, which seemed to have been turned on for the special occasion we were living through. We watched in silence and awe. Later research suggested that what we saw was a regular astronomical event, a shower of Geminid meteors usually seen around mid-December, though recent studies have revealed 'apparent activity spanning the period of November 30 to December 29'.[22]

Waiting for those hours to pass was one of the hardest times of my life. All my senses were alert and prickling, those of an animal in a state of fear, with advanced defence mechanisms running. I could hear Irene sobbing quietly but then, to my wonder, she fell asleep for a period. I couldn't imagine falling asleep facing death.

Then, new horror. I heard a car pull up at what seemed to be the house where we had sought sanctuary. A woman screamed '*No! No!*' a door slammed, and the car drove off again. Was it the young woman who had shown us the path? Was she being taken away to be interrogated and perhaps tortured? Wracked with guilt and despair, I thought to myself that, no matter how the night ended, it was impossible to go on living after this.

Gradually the sky lightened and people stirred in the distance. Irene was awake again when we heard the sound of a *bemo* approaching. It travelled slowly, emitting small toots of its horn, as the drivers do when they are circulating town streets looking for passengers. Irene whispered: 'Perhaps it *is* them. Perhaps they've come back for us.'

Her words triggered a brief pang of hope, but it was impossible to believe. They must have been arrested. But then there was a second approach. Peering cautiously through the brambles, I glimpsed a young man with long hair and a student-type satchel slung over his shoulder walking slowly past our position, whistling. Buoyed by Irene's suggestion, I decided to whistle back. It was hard, because my mouth was so dry I couldn't summon a peep at first. He replied in kind, and I stood up cautiously. Julião appeared beside him, as if from nowhere.

'We're coming to get you,' he said, 'Stay hidden until we return. Do you know where "A" is?'

'No, hasn't he been arrested?' I replied.

'I saw him down by the river, I don't know, but I think Talofo has been,' he said before disappearing.

Five minutes later the *bemo* returned, proceeding slowly and tooting as before.

'Irene, I think it's them,' I said. I showed my head above the ditch and saw a Timorese man walking behind it. He turned, saw me and beckoned, saying in Portuguese, 'Come on!'

'They've come,' I confirmed, and we emerged from the ditch together.

As we did, we were surrounded by a group of khaki-clad Kopassus soldiers, with automatic rifles slung over their shoulders and identifying insignia of rank removed. They were accompanied by a team of leather-jacketed Tonton Macoutes.

12
Capture

We were covered in brambles and dirt. They marched us up to the high road where the *bemo* was now parked, having circled round. The Timorese who had beckoned spoke to me in Portuguese. 'I'm sorry—I was also a prisoner once,' he said in explanation.

There were about 15 soldiers and INTEL agents altogether, and they clustered around the vehicle. A couple of the leather-coated agents spoke some English, and they took control. 'You must come with us,' one said, indicating that we should get in the *bemo* with all of them, 'We have to take you to our commander.'

'How far away is he?' I asked.

'A few kilometres,' he replied, 'Come!'

Although the special forces soldiers were armed, they had not pointed their guns at us so far, and we were still at the stage of persuasion, not coercion. The best that could be said for our situation was that we were still alive. The amulet given to me by the kindly cloth seller in So'e was snug in my pocket—perhaps some of his ancestors were keeping watch over us.

I had decided to try using the Timorese man, who spoke good Portuguese, as a translator, rather than speak to them directly in English. It would give more time to think and some psychological advantages. I could gauge the situation better through his words and gestures.

Irene and I spoke together softly to work out a strategy. There was no way we would enter the vehicle with these men to be driven to some distant place. The Tonton Macoutes were all in civilian dress and unidentifiable, as were the badgeless soldiers.

I realised that one of the agents was rubbing his crotch, assiduously coaxing a large erection into being, as he cast his eyes over Irene. She saw it, fear reflected on her face. It was a summons to a gang rape, probably followed by executions. We were in a grave situation.

We decided to speak very carefully, diplomatically and firmly, defending our rights in a spirited fashion, while avoiding anything that might provoke. We would refuse to be separated. There were a few Timorese in the streets now who were discreetly observing the scene.

I spoke to the translator: 'Could you please tell the gentlemen that I'm afraid we can't get in the bus with them? We are foreign citizens and would like to ring our embassies.' He did.

Before they could say anything more Irene asked them directly in English: 'Are we under arrest? What are we being charged with? Is it a crime to sleep in a ditch?' She reiterated the demand to phone embassies, a fairyland proposition given that we were miles from anywhere, and that for both of us the nearest diplomatic representation was in Jakarta. But it was important to assert our rights from the outset.

There was no response, so we conferred again. Irene suggested that we should propose that, instead of going to the military commander so many kilometres away, we could perhaps be taken under escort to the nearest Baucau hotel, and he could then be brought to us. Or we could go to Baucau police station.

We put it through the translator. There was no police station in Baucau, the INTEL replied.

They continued standing in the same positions. Stalemate. However, as the minutes passed and the conversation continued, they were losing the initiative. Reluctantly they agreed to the escort-to-hotel proposition and our curious procession of two dishevelled Western women escorted by an irregular military posse began walking slowly towards the centre of town. I doubted that there was a functioning hotel in Baucau, but it didn't matter. People could see us now, and it would be harder for our captors to commit violence.

A few hundred metres after we began walking, I spied the Baucau police station to our left. They had lied. Knowing the Indonesian police to be marginally more accountable than the military, and certainly preferable to INTEL, who were professional fingernail-pullers, we suggested in a manner as bright and naïve as we could muster, that we should wait for the commander here. At least the police were uniformed, with their ranks and names displayed clearly. We walked in the door.

One of the officers was Joaquim da Silva,[23] an East Timorese who spoke fluent, educated Portuguese, a thin man in his late 30s. He could see that we were in a distressed situation. Like many Timorese working for the Indonesian police or army, he was basically a nationalist, but needed to feed his family. They were the first to fall under suspicion when there was trouble, and needed to tread carefully at all times. They were also ill-treated and humiliated by their Indonesian superiors on occasions. His main concern was to survive, and he didn't really want to buy into this situation, but I sensed he might help in small ways—our lives were still not secure, after all.

I spoke in rapid Portuguese to exclude the Tonton Macoutes and soldiers from the conversation, explaining that we had been arrested by the military but did not wish to travel in a bus with a large armed group to an uncertain destination. He understood in a flash. We were prepared to travel to the commander in an official car with uniformed police, and no more than two men, I said—as though we were in a position to lay down the law.

He could see action was needed to save us. He busied police with our case, producing forms to fill in, which meant there was a record of our existence, making it harder for us to be spirited away without trace. A semblance of legality was being introduced into the issue. There was no point hiding my identity any longer. Finally I was no longer 'Jill Rose' or 'Jane Carlton', but could sign my real name and show my passport.

A car was brought to drive us to the commander. I asked Joaquim da Silva if he could accompany us to translate, and he agreed. It was much easier to negotiate with our captors working through Portuguese, and he was an attenuating influence. I made an effort to translate as exactly as possible to Irene, given that we could have kept to English, which would have been easier for her. In the end the car had a couple of policemen including Silva, plus two soldiers. The commander's barracks building proved to be relatively close.

It was a rectangular, one-storey office building. We were ushered into a reception area with the military guards, and offered chairs. From this position, we could see a long corridor stretching the length of the building. On each side of it were individual office-like cubicles, perhaps four or five on each side. Their doors were closed and the atmosphere was hushed. Moving regularly along the corridor was a Timorese man with a broad, flat mop. He would go into the cubicles, mop, and emerge again, also working constantly on the corridor itself. Once I saw an Indonesian in civilian dress come out of a cubicle with his hand on the shoulder of a Timorese youth, whose face betrayed no expression. They walked away and that cubicle was mopped too.

Irene and I waited there for some time, bedraggled and downcast in the company of our friendly translator and the guards. Then, from one of the end cubicles we were sitting near, the silence was broken by a strange, shuddering, violent sound. If there was a cry it was almost subliminal; it was mainly a judder, like flesh against a wall, that lasted no more than a few seconds.

We exchanged glances. The Timorese policeman looked uncomfortable. My senses moved into high alert. In the past 19 years I had been recording the histories of East Timorese torture victims, handing on all the cases I covered as a reporter to Amnesty International. They had told of electric shocks administered routinely in military barracks and other centres, with gags inserted into mouths beforehand. They had told of fingernails pulled out with pliers, of being suspended from rafters upside down for long hours as the victims were beaten with staves. I was sickeningly familiar with these places, and had even seen photos taken in cubicles such as these. Indonesian soldiers regularly took photos of victims and sold them to resistance supporters who smuggled them abroad. They were supposedly unauthorised, but because the Indonesian dictatorship and its military wing was subject to minimal international pressure for accountability, there were no constraints on it. Showing these pictures reinforced the rule of terror under which the Timorese lived and the impunity of the torturers.

We struggled to retain our composure wondering what was ahead. It was probable that 'A', Talofo and Julião were being held in those cubicles, or perhaps the young woman from the house.

We were called to the commander's office, traipsing the full length of the corridor and turning left into a wider room. On the wall were portraits of all the previous red-beret commanders of Baucau district, who seemed to have had a short shelf-life. That pesky nationalist insurgency never had gone away.

Below this gallery was a short, middle-aged, Indonesian officer with a gap between his front teeth. He grinned constantly and delivered a half-bowing greeting to us. Colonel Basrhuddin. A word slipped repeatedly into my head: 'Kempeitai, Kempeitai'. Where did a memory of Japanese secret police, World War II, come from? They too had occupied Baucau and been in the same business as this man, but I had to keep reminding myself he was Indonesian and this was 1994.

Still smiling, he showed us to some armchairs, and produced a camera. He had an English-speaking officer to translate. 'Let's take a photo for the occasion before we start!' he beamed, adopting a pose with us as his assistant raised the camera. It was a bizarre suggestion, but explained something that had puzzled me for many years. A young Timorese friend called Donaciano Gomes had been brutally tortured in a Dili prison in 1989, but when he was describing his ordeal, he produced a photo of himself with his captors, all smiling. Others had shown me similar photos. They were obligatory, it seems.

'I'm sorry, but I do not wish to have my photo taken without permission. I would like to call my ambassador, please,' Irene told him firmly but politely.

Silva translated the same message from Portuguese to Indonesian for me.

The commander continued cajoling and insisting for some time and we continued refusing in polite language.

Finally, he put the matter aside, his smile growing weaker, and began our interrogation, conducted mainly from his Indonesian, through Silva to me in Portuguese and then to English for Irene.

He asked our identities, which we gave, and then swung into a series of questions about our presence in East Timor and Baucau, who we had been with, and how we got there.

We had earlier agreed between ourselves to refuse to answer any questions except those concerning identity, on the grounds that we were foreign citizens, and with each reply we asked to be able to phone our embassies.

The colonel became increasingly annoyed at this response,

and Silva became increasingly uncomfortable, as the butt of his ire. 'Please don't ask me to translate any more. It's too difficult for me,' he pleaded. I agreed. He was a decent man, and had helped enormously. There could be repercussions later if it was pushed too far.

We made one exception to the rule of not answering questions. That was about how we got to Baucau. We were concerned that there should be no formal link between ourselves and the three Timorese who had brought us there, to avoid incriminating them at all costs, especially as we had reason to believe they were probably being held. And so I concocted a cock-and-bull story painting us as dizzy party seekers, who had met a couple of Timorese guys in Dili called Pedro and Luís, who had driven us to a party in Baucau, where they promised the beer would flow freely. We didn't know their surnames.

Colonel Basrhuddin retreated to his desk in disgust, and began shuffling papers and making phone calls. He offered use of the bathroom adjoining the office so we could clean up. Irene went first and I followed.

It was a large, *mandi*-style toilet with a tiled tank full of cool water. Our clothes were irredeemably filthy and stinking after two days in them, including the night in the ditch, but it was good to sluice some water over the body. As I opened the door to return, my eye was drawn to a patch of floor. It and part of the door-frame were spattered with blood.

We sat dejectedly with Joaquim da Silva in the hushed office, waiting to know the commander's next move. Then the sound came again from the wall of the adjoining plywood cubicle. Right next to us. Was it coming from one of our companions? It was slightly different from the previous sound, like a swift, muffled tattoo of fists beating helplessly on the wall, perhaps from a body convulsed.

Everyone in the room heard it. Silva's body tensed;

he probably heard such sounds regularly. He lowered his head, sweat on his brow, eyes evasive. The colonel heard it—maybe he planned it, so that we could hear it too. Irene and I exchanged glances. I couldn't stand it. I knew that if I rose and walked the ten or so paces to the door of the next cubicle I could stop what was happening by flinging it open and seeing what was inside, exposing the culprit. All my life I had written against torture and if I didn't take those ten steps when it most mattered I was a hypocrite, an accomplice. Irene glowered at me, willing me not to. From the outset of our ordeal we had formed a good team, counterbalancing defiance with diplomacy and doing whatever we needed to survive. I knew she was right, and that it could be our death warrant. For six months afterwards I flung that door open every night, I took those ten steps in a fever of half-wakefulness, but that day I didn't.

13
Interrogation

The commander had decided we would be transferred to Dili for further questioning. I hoped Joaquim da Silva would accompany us, but it was out of the question. We were to be accompanied by three uniformed Kopassus officers and a plain-clothed East Timor informer called Edi, one of the lowest pieces of humanity the blighted half-island had ever had to support. He was a whining opportunist who alternated between groping us and cadging cigarettes. At least the other Timorese who had led us into the *bemo* trap (whom I met again as Miguel after the 1999 Indonesian withdrawal) had the dignity to apologise and explain that he had been coerced into compliance. Even the place we collected Edi from seemed indicative: the jeep pulled in at the front door of what looked like a private house, the front room of which was packed with half-naked young East Timorese men with dead eyes. It looked like yet another Baucau torture chamber. Irene and I sat in the back with Edi and delivered him the odd kick when the soldiers weren't looking, warning him to keep away from us.

We weren't handcuffed but our status as prisoners was evident. We were led into a restaurant in Manatuto, half-way to Dili, for lunch, and Irene took the opportunity of a *mandi* visit to dispose of some half-chewed up addresses we'd both been working on.

It was late afternoon when we arrived in the capital. We were taken to POLWIL (Indonesian regional police) headquarters, where there was a new, beefed-up interrogation routine. They sat us on chairs with two uniformed INTEL officers sitting in front of us peppering us with questions. Or, rather, trying to.

Our morale was sagging by now from sheer exhaustion and because there was no indication where this was going to end. They continued to deny us the right to ring our embassies. In my case this may have been useless anyway—as a public critic of Australian foreign policy I was regarded with hostility in diplomatic circles, with a few notable exceptions. I had determined that instead of calling personally I would get Irene to ask the Dutch if they could inform the Australian embassy of my arrest.

We tried not to show any signs we were despondent, and were cheered immeasurably by the surreal conditions of the interrogation. BRIMOB, the riot police, were drilling in the yard outside, emitting animalistic war cries as they did, making it impossible for us to hear the interrogators or them to hear us. They were jumping and leaping collectively in martial arts poses, grunting sounds like 'Haaaa! Eeeeee!' and 'Aaaakkk!' As if this din wasn't bad enough, the afternoon monsoon set in with thunderous rain drumming on the corrugated iron roof. The Dili interrogators were almost as irritated as the Baucau commander and we continued stubbornly to refuse to answer anything beyond our names, nationalities and addresses. We asked continually what they were charging us with and when we could call Jakarta.

One thing did become clear: that INTEL had an extensive file on our expedition before we set foot on the island. They appeared to have our entire itinerary. An informer in resistance ranks had betrayed us—perhaps one of the Dili operatives who had been told we were Indonesian agents. That person couldn't be blamed, but the source could.

During our interrogation a general in full uniform looked in, and another officer, whom I recognised as the man sitting behind me with the floppy tennis cap on the Kefamenanu bus. Our case had obviously attracted senior attention.

After an hour or so of questions, there was a breakthrough. A man in standard Tonton Macoute sunglasses arrived from the immigration department. He was Peter Timbul, the deputy director of immigration in Dili, and he was fully aware who we were. We had ascertained from the interrogators that under Indonesian law they could hold us for something like two days without charge but would then be forced to free us, in theory.

He examined my passport. It was now 1 December 1994 and the disguise adopted in June had faded, with hair colour reverting to normal and glasses discarded. He pointed to the photo in the newly acquired passport and asked why it didn't resemble me, suggesting the document was a forgery and then made some reference to my entrance to Indonesia through Medan. He insinuated that both of us were linked to the Timorese military resistance and might be charged with security offences, to be held indefinitely pending investigation.

I felt pale at this turn of events. He announced that we would be transferred into the custody of the immigration authorities and drove us to their building a short distance away.

But there we met his superior, Johannes Sri Triswoyo, who was a completely different character. At first his Ray-Bans and appearance suggested he too was from INTEL. He looked like a Tonton Macoute, smelt like a Tonton Macoute and at times acted like one, but from his demeanour and conversation I became sure he wasn't. He was a Christian from Jogjakarta, a Protestant. Contrary to the aggressive stance of Timbul, he announced that he had been in conference with his superiors in Jakarta and had decided to free us. We were to be expelled from East Timor, although not from Indonesia, a measure we were to understand better later.

One of the wire services had published a tiny story saying that two foreign journalists, 'Irene Slegt and Jill Rose', had been arrested in Baucau. It had been published in the *Jakarta Post*, where Pascal Mallet of France-Presse had spotted it. He then published a large story identifying me as one of the journalists concerned, who had followed the Timor story for many years and was a respected authority on the issue. I was most grateful—a story like that when a reporter is in strife can often influence the outcome positively, and it definitely helped.

The immigration director offered use of his phone and left the room while Irene spoke to the first secretary at the Dutch embassy who proved extremely sympathetic. He invited her to stay with him when she arrived in Jakarta and briefed her on her legal rights. The Indonesians no longer had power to detain us, he said, and we could ask to go to a hotel.

Irene put this to Triswoyo and he agreed it was correct legally, but suggested we not go to a hotel. 'I think you should sleep in my office,' he said, 'I'll organise beds and give you a key so you can lock it from the inside. The INTEL are not happy with me. They want me to lock you in the immigration cells, but I won't. If you go to a hotel they might come and take you away.'

He then invited us to his home for a cool drink and a bath but before we left the office some military intelligence officers called in. Throughout our detention we had avoided having our bags searched. They realised they'd forgotten, and had decided to do so belatedly. Irene had her video camera there, and incriminating tape of the Timorese underground in Jakarta. However, we were in Triswoyo's custody now. He asked if we wanted our bags searched. 'No,' we replied baldly, a decision that Triswoyo said must be respected. The visitors then asked Irene whether she had a camera in her bag, to which she replied, 'No,' just as baldly. They left empty-handed.

We were embarrassed to be introduced to his demure wife and young son in the state we were in. It took a long time to get the dirt off, and then we had to step back into the foul clothes we had been wearing, but our host cheered us up by promising to take us shopping for new clothes the next day. He had already requisitioned plane seats to Bali, which we paid for.

Over a cold beer after we cleaned up, Triswoyo tried to prise some information from us about why we had been in Baucau, and what we were doing. It was not hostile questioning but we feared for our Timorese companions, and besides, he was part of the Indonesian government apparatus. Any information that provided an incriminating link to them had to be avoided. They were, no doubt, in deep trouble already.

He confided to us that Timbul was jealous of him because he had a degree, and he was an uneducated man. He wanted to run the show, he stressed. It seemed the nearest he could come to telling us that Timbul was the INTEL hatchet man in the Dili immigration department.

He said also that military intelligence had refused to share our file with him, which was unusual. But he did tell us that the place where we had been hiding was reputed to have been used as an ambush point by David Alex and his guerrillas in the past. This could explain why they seemed to know where we were but made no attempt to drag us out. They feared there might be armed people in there with us.

We chatted until nightfall and he then took us to dinner at a Dili karaoke bar, driving us to his office later. His staff had made up two neat beds with clean sheets. He gave us the key, saying, 'You must lock yourselves in here and don't open the door to anyone, even if you know them. I will come to get you for breakfast first thing.'

As he stood in the doorway I heard a long, unearthly

scream come from somewhere close by, a scream like I never want to hear again. It jolted me, and I suddenly felt confused about Triswoyo, and whether it was right to trust him. Weren't they his immigration cells nearby? It was important to me to find a righteous Indonesian, and my gut feeling had been that Triswoyo was it. I didn't want to be disillusioned.

Irene and I settled to sleep. At about 1 am there was a knock on the door. We saw the shapes of people outside, and kept silent. The knock was repeated. 'It's Peter Timbul,' a voice said, 'Let me in. I need to talk to you.' We ignored him and sometime later they went away.

Triswoyo came and collected us for breakfast in the morning as agreed. By this time we had packed up our bedding and Timorese staff had begun arriving at the office. When he came he sat behind his desk. He then introduced me to one of the Timorese, who he had earlier greeted in a warm fashion. 'One day, he will sit in this chair,' he told us. Pushing him further for the meaning of this statement I asked: 'Where will you be then?' He smiled, but didn't answer. Later he asked me: 'What do you really think of East Timor?' I paused to consider my answer carefully because I thought he deserved it. 'I think it's the saddest land on earth,' I replied.

Over breakfast at his house, he presented me with a small, formal letter that said something like: 'Dear Miss Jill, I would be most grateful if you could please tell me, just for personal reasons, why you were in the ditch?' Despite earlier doubts, I had decided that Triswoyo was trustworthy and that maybe he was my righteous Indonesian. I felt a certain sadness for his small family. They were people trying to introduce a little humanity into a basically unjust situation, but nevertheless were part of an occupation force. If there was a backlash, such nuances would not be remembered: history would just remember them as part of it. However, the safety of our companions couldn't be risked. I looked up from his letter, saying, 'I'm really sorry, but I can't tell you now. One day in the future, but not now.'

On 1 December 1994 we were taken around Dili under escort, to the curious stares of the East Timorese. First we bought new clothes, and then Triswoyo allowed us to call friends from public phones at the post office.

One thing that worried us greatly was whether Malla had been caught in Bali. If not, we had to warn her. We also needed to try and get plane bookings directly out of Indonesia from Bali as soon after we landed as possible.

I didn't want to ring Malla's partner Mark directly in case he gave an emotional response on the phone, which might give something away, as the phones were undoubtedly tapped. So I rang my friend Judy McLean in Sydney, telling her we were under arrest and indicating in the most guarded language possible that she should ring Mark and break the news that Malla might be in danger and that he should contact her to leave immediately.

I also asked her to move heaven and earth to book a seat on a plane from Denpasar to Sydney that evening, as we would be arriving in Bali in late afternoon and needed to quit Indonesia quickly. Irene made a similar call to her partner Simon Long in Hong Kong. He was also a journalist, so wasn't all that perturbed to hear that Irene had been arrested challenging yet another dictatorship, although he couldn't know then how close she had come to death.

On hearing the news, Mark immediately rang the villa in Bali. Malla was still free. Before our departure we had joked about code names we might adopt for our undercover assignment, and Mark and Malla had laughingly said I could be dubbed 'Auntie'. I was furious, being sensitive about any reference to my advancing age. Now the pseudonym proved useful: 'Auntie's sick!' he told her, 'You must come home immediately.' Somehow she managed to collect together the massive pile of luggage for three people and check out and pay up, saying she had a dying relative in Australia. She was on a plane out of Indonesia within two hours of the call. Her involvement was never discovered, and for us she became The Third Woman, production assistant extraordinaire.

Triswoyo was visibly worried over the plan to escort us to the airport. The immigration department had paltry resources in comparison to INTEL, which was a direct part of the military, and he trusted only himself. (Timbul was part of INTEL but was nominally immigration. Under the Indonesian system, INTEL agents were assigned undercover to all government departments and were ranking military officers, usually from Kopassus.)

When the moment came, they used two vans. Triswoyo drove the first with us in the back with a couple of other officers. Timbul drove the escort van accompanied by another officer and communicating with Triswoyo by radio. Irene and I were only ushered out of the immigration building after Triswoyo had done a thorough visual check up and down the road. The basis of his fears were not clear. Did he think we would escape, or that the resistance might try to free us, or that there would be demonstrations? Or was it that INTEL might interfere in some negative way? I calculated that the last was the probable reason, and this assumption was borne out by the fact that as we proceeded we could see men with Ray-Bans and radios lining the streets for the entire route, about 100 metres apart. They were not immigration officials.

Irene and I were both deeply depressed. Not only had this half-baked adventure ended in journalistic failure, personal disaster and almost got us killed, but to the best of our knowledge good people who helped us had been arrested and were probably being put to torture—they didn't have the option of repatriation. The fact that all of this may have resulted from the work of a resistance informer, of uncertain identity, made our plight seem even bleaker.

Immersed in these black thoughts, suddenly we became aware of a commotion behind us. We turned and saw that a carload of young Timorese men and women had swung in behind us and were shouting, '*Viva os jornalistas! Viva Timor-Leste independente!*' (Long live the journalists! Long live independent East Timor!), cheering us and punching clenched fists in the air. They continued for a short distance and then turned off and sped away. It was a moving gesture, in which they risked all to send us a message of support under the very noses of INTEL.

At the airport we were taken to a VIP lounge and served a meal while Timbul and Triswoyo sat with us until it was time to board the flight. From the window we saw a group of about six uniformed officers leave another building. 'Who are they?' Irene asked. 'They're from the military VIP section,' Timbul replied, 'They're on the same flight as you.'

Triswoyo took us onto the tarmac. He shook the hands of each of us in turn, saying, 'You're being expelled from Timor, but not from Indonesia. I'm afraid I can't protect you after this.'

As we walked towards the plane, which was the normal Garuda flight to Bali, the military officers who had been standing to one side also moved off, walking ahead of us. As they neared the stairs, they swung round. Most had cameras in their hands, which they thrust relentlessly in our faces, clicking, clicking, against our protests—finally, they had the photos we had refused. We broke free like film stars fleeing from paparazzi, flinging scarves over our faces and running panic-stricken up the stairs of the plane, which they also mounted. Once inside they took their seats as though nothing had happened.

The pair of us were seated towards the front. Irene was on one side of me and a well-dressed man who looked like a Chinese-Timorese businessman was to the other. It was then that I began to display the first signs of mental disintegration. I pointed to his watch and said to Irene in a loud voice: 'Look, he's working for INTEL—have a look at this Rolex watch!' I repeated it. As Irene attempted to hush me, the poor man moved quietly to another seat in embarrassment.

14
The Holiday Inn Siege

We were relieved to land in Bali. It seemed the ordeal was over and we would soon be safely home. Our first priority was to telephone Judy and Simon to see if we had a connecting flight that night.

As we filed out of the arrivals lounge, a man standing behind a desk near the door asked to see our passports. We showed them, and he introduced himself as head of airport security in Denpasar. It was late afternoon and the air on our face as we came out of the building was hot and humid. There was a row of small street stalls where hawkers sold snacks, and a newspaper seller. Afternoon light was giving way to evening. We found the public telephones and began dialling. It took a while to get through. We were both aghast to find that we could not travel that day—the earliest flights available were next afternoon. We would have to sleep the night in Bali. Although we had paid-up air tickets out of the country, we had almost no cash left for a hotel. We continued phoning, trying to find something cheap and, as we did, I noticed a large, unshaven man with a silk batik shirt moving up to Irene with a pistol sticking out of his belt. It was dark near these phones, which were a little removed from the main illuminated area outside the arrivals lounge. Another man banged against me as he walked past, as if by accident, also making a point of showing a weapon under his shirt. They looked like real thugs. I hung up and alerted Irene. We moved to a brightly-lit airport café to think and talk over a drink. We could see the pair of them leering in, and soon they were joined by the so-called security officer and the newspaper seller.

We decided that our best course was to book into a five-star hotel, barricade ourselves into the room, using only room service for meals, and working the telephones for help. We would call our embassies and request diplomatic protection. We didn't have enough money between us to book in even for a night, but I called Judy again, and she offered to send a fax to the management guaranteeing payment of all costs.

The next problem was how to get there. There was a group of international hotels close to the airport, but we were afraid of walking there with this gang on our tail. Triswoyo's last words to us had new meaning.

I didn't want to end up like Marsinah, a 25-year-old Indonesian trade union activist whose body had been found in a village on Java in May 1993. Workers involved in a strike at her factory had been ordered to appear at the local army barracks and threatened. Some were dismissed from their jobs. Marsinah was snatched from the street after visiting a friend alone one evening. A post-mortem found that she had died of injuries inflicted as a result of torture. She had been severely beaten, suffering wounds to her neck, both wrists and internal haemorrhages. She was then raped and her body dumped.

We eventually solved the problem of how to get to a hotel when we realised that the Holiday Inn, which was only a few hundred metres away, had a pick-up bus driving a regular circle route past the airport concourse. We would wait until the last moment to hail it and pile in. This worked but by the time we got to the hotel the thugs had re-assembled outside the front gate, and their numbers had grown—other street hawkers had also transmuted into Tonton Macoutes.

We were given a twin room by an attendant in a neat Holiday Inn uniform, and settled to rest and talk for a while. It was too late to call embassies—we would do that in the morning—and we called room service for dinner. It took a long time to come, but when it did, it was served by the former head of airport security in a Holiday Inn uniform. The harassment escalated by the hour. Later on, another person in hotel uniform knocked. We reluctantly opened the door when he said he had come to repair the lock. We concurred because security was foremost in our minds, but then realised the lock wasn't broken. He stood in the half-open door, fiddling with it casually and watching us for as long as possible before leaving. From all appearances, INTEL had requisitioned the Holiday Inn.

It was difficult to sleep, and we spent most of the night analysing events since the chase began on the outskirts of Baucau. We discussed whether one of the three in our car had been working for INTEL, Julião being the obvious suspect. The soldiers must have been standing nearby when he spoke to me by the roadside—how else could they have appeared so quickly? But perhaps this was judging him unfairly; anything was possible in the world of East Timor, where reality had been distorted beyond recognition. It seemed certain that some of those in the car had been arrested and taken to the Kopassus barracks. People from the household that had begged us to leave may also have been arrested. How could we live with this?

Throughout history reprisals have been exercised against innocent people to deter acts of political or practical support for those fighting against tyranny. Guilt is invoked to prevent repetition of such acts. The Nazis had burnt whole villages, or tortured whole groups of people, because one person had hidden an Allied airman, or smuggled goods or weapons to partisans fighting in the hills. Who could live with responsibility for so many deaths, so much torture? How could such guilt be endured?

The answer, it seemed to me, was to reject the terms of this sick logic altogether. If everybody rejected it, reprisals would be ineffective. I knew the calibre of the East Timorese, who for two decades had fought a near-miraculous resistance war. Their courage was almost bottomless. I had interviewed many victims of appalling torture. Some had spoken in their pain, which was understandable. A majority endured it. In both categories they willingly returned to fight against the occupation at the first opportunity, knowing they could be tortured again. I once met a man in Lisbon who told me that, in the very early days of their struggle, he had been viciously tortured by INTEL after they had produced a copy of one of my books and pointed to his photo in it. 'Do you regret that I wrote it?' I asked him. 'Never, I'm glad you did,' he said.

The only way to make sense of the experience we had been through, I decided, was to finish the film at any cost, to go on as before. Santana would have agreed. Life might be a bit rough from now on. I had never cared much for niceties, now I didn't care at all. I would just do what I felt necessary for the Timorese until the war ended. All the signs were that there were only a few more years to go.

Next morning Irene rang the Dutch first secretary in Jakarta and asked if he could organise a diplomatic car to take her to her flight. We were surrounded in the hotel, she explained. The thugs were no longer just surrounding the hotel—now it was our room. When we awoke from our few hours of restless sleep and pulled back the curtains, we discovered that there seemed to be an entire work party of INTELs. There were men endlessly scrubbing a boardwalk outside, going up and down, time and again. Some were communicating with radios.

The Dutch sympathised and agreed to escort Irene to her flight, which departed a couple of hours before mine. I rang the Australians, who no doubt had been following my progress closely. I explained that, having been arrested in Timor and expelled, I was now being followed and harrassed by unknown armed men in Bali and asked would it be possible for a diplomat to escort me from the hotel to the airport. 'We've got a priority Medi-vac case from Denpasar airport today, but I'll see if I can spare someone to come and have a chat with you,' came the reluctant answer.

Half an hour later an Australian consular official knocked on the door. I outlined the problem to him, and explained that we weren't safe even in the hotel because the Indonesian secret police seemed to have mounted an entire operation to intimidate us. It was probably only psycho-terror, but we were concerned there could be a physical attack too.

He seemed to consider this a rather surprising claim, and to be unaware that Indonesia even had a secret police. 'I'll look around and get back to you,' he said. Not long after, he returned. 'I've spoken to hotel authorities,' he said, 'and there seems to be nothing untoward going on here. Sorry, we can't help you.' I didn't think he would understand if I told him it was probably the secret police he had spoken to.

I was now in the position of being left totally unprotected after Irene's flight left. I telephoned Judy in Australia. She had already contacted SBS Television, who had asked the Department of Foreign Affairs and Trade to act over my plight. She said she would try to increase pressure on DFAT, but neither of us were confident of getting satisfactory protection, because of my history. This didn't alter the fact that I was an Australian citizen whose rights diplomats were paid to defend to the fullest possible extent. Then she remembered that she had a friend with a daytime radio show, and that it might be possible to have me interviewed live on ABC radio from the hotel room.

Around four hours before my plane was due to take off, I was on air. 'Can you describe the scene to me at the Holiday Inn?' the interviewer asked. I gave the history of our landing in Denpasar after the Timor ordeal, the unknown men with guns, the mounting psychological harassment, and the Australian consul's refusal to assist. The Dutch had agreed with my colleague Irene Slegt that her life might be in danger, I pointed out, and were offering her every protection. The interview sounded pretty dramatic, reflecting my doomed outlook, and I even threw in mention of a helicopter now hovering near our room, which probably had nothing to do with us, but certainly heightened my anxiety.

Thirty minutes later I had a call from the consulate to say they'd changed their mind and someone would be there to take me to the plane.

Irene departed to safety. She would be met in Jakarta by embassy staff, and would be sleeping in the residence, leaving from there to Hong Kong the next day. The Dutch were keen for her to give a detailed briefing of what she had seen in East Timor and the events in Denpasar, as any conscientious diplomats with an honest political agenda would be. The Australians had not the slightest interest. But perhaps they didn't need a briefing—their surveillance base near Darwin was so sophisticated that it could just about pick up the screams in Timorese prisons.

The consul came in a white Mercedes. There was a certain satisfaction in seeing the disappointed look on the faces of the Tonton Macoutes as I sailed by. I was tempted to do an Elizabeth II-style wave but resisted anything that might provoke a reaction. I still wasn't out of Indonesia. The diplomat escorted me to a restricted area of the Qantas office while he dealt with the formalities of my exit. My tormentors ran up from the Holiday Inn, soon gathering outside the Qantas door. It was only after I was escorted right through customs that I could begin to feel safe. Like a guardian angel Judy had used her travel industry contacts to obtain an upgrade of my seat to first class. I lay back and tried to forget the past few days for a brief period.

15
Mending Broken Pieces

In August 2008, 14 years after I heard that midnight scream from the ditch in Baucau, I was in Dili face to face with Adolfo Belo, whose forced departure in an INTEL car had triggered it. His wife Benvinda Rodrigues had uttered the scream, which was followed by the sound of a door slamming and the car speeding off.

I had asked him to meet with me under the mediation of Dona Mira Martins da Silva, director of PRADET, a Timorese organisation working to heal the psychosocial damage inflicted by the Indonesian occupation. Her knowledge of the effects of post-traumatic stress on her compatriots was expert. I thought she would be an ideal mediator and she accepted the role readily. I was not disappointed.

By the time I had flown out of Bali in December 1994 to safety in Sydney I was disintegrating psychologically. The strain of weeks of hiding and living in fear of arrest, our capture in Baucau and the Alice in Wonderland-style tricks played by INTEL's practitioners of psycho-terror at the airports of Dili and Denpasar had taken their toll. The anger that began eating at me after my capture, stemming from the belief that resistance operatives had betrayed our expedition, was perhaps more destructive.

The signs of breakdown had appeared earlier in the journey, of which one example was the accusation that the Chinese businessman on the Dili–Bali flight was a police agent. It was a paranoid delusion; by that stage I could no longer distinguish between friends and enemies.

In Sydney I should have felt safe, as I was among friends: Judy, Mark, Malla and SBS's Greg Wilesmith, but the problem resurfaced when I visited a bank in Martin Place with Mark and Malla to close the account we had set up for the film production.

As I entered, I noticed some Asian people taking photographs around the entrance, and immediately assumed that Indonesia's INTEL was still following me in Australia, a thought that soon ran out of control. Within minutes I was accosting and berating an Asian man waiting in a teller's queue. 'I know you're following me, this is Australia, you can't do this here!' I shrieked as he shrank from me. My friends' alarmed response brought me back to reality and the realisation that I was in some sort of meltdown. My unsuspecting victims were most likely tourists, who abounded in Martin Place. I fled in embarrassment. Greg later took me to his family doctor, who prescribed sedatives and a good sleep.

In the following period I returned home to Portugal and for the next six months was plagued by some of the classical symptoms of post-traumatic stress disorder. It was rare to sleep more than four hours a night and if I did, it might be to wake screaming as nightmare shards dissolved, eluding memory.

In waking hours I re-lived the period in the ditch and in the Kopassus barracks countless times, endlessly mulling over the evidence of betrayal. In the streets of Lisbon I looked over my shoulder for pursuers and, far from the determined investigator who had set out on the journey to find Santana, I had become a person almost afraid of her own shadow, diminished and weak, trusting no-one.

I was sustained by one thing: the pledge made during the Holiday Inn siege to show the meaninglessness of reprisals by completing the aborted film.

I had told *Dateline* that despite much of the AU$40,000 budget having been spent before our arrest, I would find a way to finish the film and deliver it. (This was foolish perhaps, because freelance filmmakers who have been arrested, imprisoned or suffered trauma in such circumstances sometimes plead *force majeure* and are excused of the debt.) It took two years of knocking on the doors of film and television producers before I found a new financier in Portugal's RTP (Radiotelevisão Portuguesa), a state-run channel.

I could no longer cross an Indonesian border, so worked out a scheme to pay an independent camera operator to do the filming, whose work I could direct by long-distance telephone contact. Since 1994 the guerrillas had acquired satellite phones from supporters, and by this means I planned to guide the reporter's journey from Bangkok.

Dom Rotheroe was a British cinematographer who had scored a recent success with a documentary on Bosnia called *A Sarajevo Diary*. He was keen to go to East Timor and liked the project. I met him in London and prepared interview questions in Portuguese for him to carry in to the guerrilla commanders, complete with basic instructions on how to behave on camera (never look into the camera unless instructed, behave naturally, for example).

Once Dom was on the ground in Timor I dialled in to their satellite phone system, talking regularly with the commanders running operations in the east.

During Dom's final briefing in Bangkok before departure I had discussed with him the option of filming a combat operation with the guerrillas if this occurred in the normal course of events. I stressed that this was not being asked of him; it was not a condition of the contract and I would not ask of him anything I hadn't done myself, but it was important that he think beforehand about what he would do if the situation arose. I had asked him at the initial interview in London whether or not he had combat experience as a camera operator, to which he replied that he had come under fire in Sarajevo. I am not sure that this was adequate preparation for the experience he eventually had in accompanying the guerrillas on an ambush of Indonesian soldiers launched from a roadside hill near Venilale, south of Baucau. As the first shots rang out his camera swung wildly to the sky before he was able to resume control but, in filming the pre-battle briefing by commanders David Alex and Taur Matan Ruak to exhort their troops to be courageous, he obtained rare and moving footage, and when he settled down during the battle there were also some very special shots of David Alex fearlessly confronting enemy fire.

Completing the film was not easy. To begin with, all of Dom's courageous work was in danger of being lost because the tapes had been entrusted to the wrong courier and left with a Timorese network in Bali, which refused to hand them over. It was only after F.F. obtained a letter from Xanana ordering them to hand it to our courier that they did so.

I collected them from a new courier called 'Akita' in Singapore. I first had to spring him from the clutches of immigration officials who had arrested him over a currency issue—he needed to be carrying US dollars to enter. They did not search him and let him make a phone call. When I heard of his detention my blood ran cold at the thought that his precious cargo might be discovered and seized. Some serious theatricals were called for: I freed him with an unlikely story of being a kindly aunt from Lisbon who was taking him sightseeing in Singapore.

The problems continued in the post-production phase, with both *Dateline* and the Portuguese channel RTP, with whom it was now contracted, imposing tight financial conditions. The final edit was done in Lisbon where RTP claimed ownership of the tapes.

The result was *Blockade*, the only documentary shot behind guerrilla lines during the 24-year occupation, which became a cult film among the East Timorese after the Indonesian withdrawal.

✣ ✣ ✣ ✣ ✣

With time my trauma symptoms receded. In September 1999 I re-entered East Timor with the second intake of the UN's armed peacekeeping force (InterFET) and resumed work as a foreign correspondent.

What should have been a triumphal return was tinged with sadness. Nino Konis Santana had not lived to see the liberation he had fought for in such heroic conditions. He died unexpectedly in March 1998, just 18 months before the UN-sponsored referendum of 30 August 1999.

The official story put out by the resistance was that his death was caused by injuries sustained from a fall while on the march in the mountainous Ainaro district.

Another journalist had visited him sometime after me and I had seen brief television images of Santana at his Mirtutu base, in which his appearance shocked me. He had been in poor health when I was with him, but now his face looked puffy and was covered with a film of sweat. His health appeared to have deteriorated.

For this reason I doubted the resistance's characteristically heroic version of his death. I was in Lisbon at the time and efforts to check my sources from that distance failed. In the absence of an alternative version I had to base the obituary I wrote on the official version, while treating it with caution.

At the first opportunity to get out of Dili after returning with InterFET I travelled to Lete-foho in the hope of finding and thanking those who helped me reach Santana. I found Senhora Arranhado, who had hidden me. Their family had assisted Australian troops against the Japanese during World War II, and I knew her son António, who had arrived in Lisbon after fleeing the Santa Cruz massacre.

The family had told António of assisting me, in a letter

or phone call, but I feigned ignorance when he had come to me smilingly with this knowledge. War was still under way in East Timor and I had sworn not to reveal identities to anyone, so wasn't going to make an exception. I lied to my young friend.

I found his mother with a group of people and they all welcomed me back. I thanked them for their sacrifices, and asked them how exactly Santana had died. They told me that, when they descended to his bunker to wake him for breakfast, he was slumped dead against the wall, with liquid coming from his mouth, clear, not blood.

He had possibly been suffering from tuberculosis, as many of the mountain fighters did, but the bullets in his chest and neck had been there for a long period, and may have moved or been poisoning him slowly.

In his 2005 biography of Santana, Portuguese historian José Mattoso wrote:

> A certain mystery surrounds this death. From an historic viewpoint, there seems no reason for it. A reading of his correspondence shows that his life was often in danger during the many battles he fought, or was threatened by serious illnesses, and that his living conditions, shut away in a poorly-aired bunker for long periods, were unhealthy.[24]

The speculation in East Timor about the circumstances seems to have more to do with the fact that Nino Konis Santana was the only Fataluku person to have led the guerrilla resistance. The Fatalukus of the eastern Lospalos region are a proud ethnic minority who speak one of the few Papuan-based languages of East Timor and are subject to discrimination when they venture west to Dili in search of work. It was natural for Konis's supporters to grasp at conspiracy theories over a death for which contradictory explanations had been given.

Mattoso gives an explanation for the story told in the

press release. It is that after his body was found in the Mirtutu bunker, he was buried secretly at night and a statement released that was designed to take the focus from the Lete-foho area by creating the story that he had died on military duties in the Ainaro district. The resistance feared the Indonesian army would try to seize the body. If the peaceful death in Mirtutu was mentioned it could lead them not only to the body, but to the discovery of his hideout and arrest of those who had supported him.[25]

In this period I also travelled to Baucau and found Benvinda. I expressed my sorrow for all she and her family had suffered because of their chance contact with us in 1994.

Although the nightmares had faded, my behaviour was erratic, swinging between withdrawal and bouts of unpredictable anger; good people became victims of my unprovoked withering sarcasm. Where it came from, I had no idea, but I guessed it was seeping out from the untreated problems of 1994. After a bout of depression in 2006 I sought help.

It took another two years before I found Dr John Cooper, a Melbourne specialist in post-traumatic stress disorder.

The meeting with Adolfo and another later with his wife Benvinda went ahead under Dona Mira's supervision in Dili, with Dr Cooper accompanying the process from Melbourne after a series of weekly consultations at which he had confirmed a diagnosis of post-traumatic stress disorder.

Since 1994 I had avoided examining seriously the events in Baucau that night; now I felt I needed to know the worst of what happened to those arrested, to demystify the whole event, in order to deal with it rationally. My imagination had reconstructed all sorts of scenarios about the woman who screamed, who I imagined had been seized herself.

Dr Cooper had welcomed my initiative, as a form of *in vivo* therapy, which would help me confront one source of my disorder (guilt/shame over Adolfo and Benvinda's suffering) in a personal encounter with those involved. I sent him an email report from Dili on the outcomes.

I did not keep notes of either of the meetings, so the account that follows may not be exact. This is because it was a charged occasion and I did not feel capable of writing while I was experiencing the strong emotions involved, and I did not want to treat Adolfo and Benvinda as mere objects for my writing. We needed to discuss our feelings fully across the table on a mutual, human basis.

At the counselling session at PRADET Adolfo confirmed that it was indeed Benvinda's scream I had heard. He told me that he and his father had been arrested and taken to the Kopassus barracks. They were subject to vicious torture, but with the help of a friendly guard he had escaped in the early hours of the morning and fled to Dili to hide. He was safe in the short-term, but was to suffer more over the event in the future. It was painful for him to speak and his face contorted with emotion at times, his voice quavering with tears. I told him how deeply sorry I was to be associated with his suffering. He had at first been uncertain of my motives in asking to speak to him, but by now he understood.

'Please don't blame yourself,' he told me, 'to me winning independence wiped out all that suffering. I have my reward, and we are honoured to have helped you.'

Some weeks later I had a similar session at PRADET with Benvinda. She had been tortured in Baucau during an earlier, unrelated period of imprisonment, but on this occasion she remained free. After Adolfo had been imprisoned and fled, she came home one evening to find that INTEL had visited her house to leave a message of terror. It had been ransacked, a dog butchered there and its blood and entrails smeared on the wall.

From Benvinda's testimony I learnt of Adolfo's re-arrest at a house in Dili, where incriminating pieces of the luggage Irene and I abandoned in jumping from the car in Baucau were found. He was imprisoned and tortured for a substantial period.

Released on parole, he was obliged to report weekly to Indonesian police. He was in such a wretched psychological and physical state that he told Benvinda he would not be reporting to the police. They decided to hide out. They built a shanty in one of the new settlements at Becora on the outskirts of Dili and hid successfully until the war ended.

Epilogue

These were the things that happened to me and two of the Timorese involved in the journey to find Santana. Others who were part of the journey suffered the varying fortunes typical of those who lived through East Timor's recent history.

Irene Slegt published *Bitter Dawn* (2002), as Irene Crystalis, containing an account of our November 1994 journey. We later disagreed over her claim that I had consented to a proposal for guerrillas to stage an ambush for filming but she withdrew the allegations in her 2009 version of the book, *East Timor: A Nation's Bitter Dawn* (2009). She continues to report on human rights issues.

'The Third Woman', Malla Nunn, switched from film-making to runaway success as a writer of thrillers set in her native Africa, creating the character of Detective Emmanuel Cooper in *A Beautiful Place to Die* (2009) and *Let the Dead Lie* (2010).

After my return to East Timor in 1999, I came across Joaquim da Silva and Miguel on separate occasions. Both said that the INTEL agents had discussed killing Irene Slegt and me after our capture.

F.F., real name Avelino Coelho da Silva, became Secretary of State for Energy in the Parliamentary Alliance Majority (AMP) government of Xanana Gusmão in 2007.

Natan, real name Hernani Coelho da Silva, became The Democratic Republic of East Timor's Ambassador to Australia from 2006 to 2009 and was then appointed chief-of-staff of President José Ramos Horta's external delegation.

Child courier Natalino Coelho da Silva survived the war and trained as a diplomat after independence but did not take up the option. He instead emigrated to the UK to work in a Liverpool factory.

Tommy, real name Tomé Jeronimo, never lost his sense of humour or critical spirit. Today he is a Commissioner for the National Electoral Commission.

Benvinda Rodrigues became a member of parliament for the CNRT party in the same government.

Adolfo Belo works for the recognition of the ex-guerrillas and torture survivors who fought for East Timor's independence.

Akita, who had carried the footage of *Blockade* from Timor to Singapore, faced a death sentence in a Dili court. He was arrested in 1997 while disembarking from a passenger ferry, allegedly with bombs in his bag. He was sentenced to 20 years but soon escaped from Becora prison and became a guerrilla fighter until the war's end, when he became a union activist. In 2007 he emigrated to the UK to work in a factory.

Like Comandante Konis, Suno Moris did not live to see independence. He was killed in combat in 1995.

Zely, real name Nuno Fernandes, became an internal refugee in the independent nation he fought to create, living in an IDP (internally displaced persons) camp after the ethnic violence of 2006. In 2007 Minister Avelino found him work as his chauffeur.

Comandante Dudo, real name Dudo Fernandes, survived the war and returned to his home in Gleno, Ermera district, to grow coffee and breed horses. There in a small alcove he has photos of my meeting with Konis Santana in Mirtutu.

Virgílio Guterres pursued his career as a journalist after release from Cipinang prison and went on to become director of East Timor's state-run TVTL television network.

After reading an account of my and Irene Slegt's arrest ordeal, a leading Timorese militant in Lisbon privately apologised to me for providing false information, with others, for the article published in *Diário de Notícias* in mid-1994.

The Tibar boat that was to have taken me and Irene Slegt past the Dili checkpoint was used a year later to bring the first Timorese 'boat people' to Australia. They included our *estafeta* António Pinto Gouveia ('A') and former child soldier Alfredo Reinado and his family. Reinado was killed in an alleged assassination attempt against President José Ramos Horta in February 2008. Ballistic evidence presented at the Dili trial of the would-be assassins suggested he had been executed.

Notes

1 Tomé Pires, *The Suma Oriental of Tomé Pires: an Account of the East, from the Red Sea to Japan, written in Malacca and India in 1512–1515 and The Book of Francisco Rodrigues: Rutter of a Voyage in the Red Sea, Nautical Rules, Almanack and Maps, Written and Drawn in the East before 1515*, p. 137.
2 Ibid, p. 139.
3 Anna Forbes, *Unbeaten Tracks in Islands of the Far East: Experiences of a Naturalist's Wife in the 1880s* (Oxford University Press, Singapore, 1989). In Susan Morgan's *Place Matters: Gendered Geography in Victorian Women's Travel Books about Southeast Asia* (Rutgers University Press, New Brunswick, 1996), the author offers a narrow feminist analysis of Anna Forbes's journal. For example, she describes Anna's decision to remain behind in a bamboo hut in the hamlet of Fatunaba in the foothills above Dili while her husband Henry explores Timorese kingdoms in the mountainous interior as 'a straightforward representation of the subjectivity prescribed for the colonial woman by Victorian imperial ideology', p. 83. Mrs Forbes's independent spirit and courage is downplayed.
4 Ibid, p. 36.
5 Op. cit., p. 295.
6 Local mini-bus, highly decorated and fitted with a sound system, usually playing heavy metal rock music; can be hired for long journeys.
7 Term used for the brutal secret police in Haiti formed in 1959 to serve dictator Jean-Claude Duvalier (known as 'Baby Doc'). The Tonton Macoutes featured in Graham Greene's novel *The Comedians.*

8 Indonesian for 'post' as in 'police post'.
9 'Maubere' is a name common to Timorese peasants, which had been converted to a term of nationalist pride—and Domingos Soares's nickname.
10 Interview with Nino Konis Santana, Mirtutu, East Timor, 12 August 1994.
11 Interview with Suno Moris, Mirtutu, 12 August 1994.
12 Interview with Konis Santana, op. cit.
13 Among those he listed were battalions 726, 723, 415, 512, 223, 316, 712, 744, 745 and 743, the engineering battalion Zipur and the territorial militia units Team Sera, Team Seca, Team Alfa and Team Makikit.
14 Today commander of East Timor's new army, with the rank of Major-General.
15 Interview with Konis Santana, op. cit.
16 Ibid.
17 In 2006 Mr Alatas, then retired as foreign minister, published a book bearing these words. At the launch of *The Pebble in the Shoe: The Diplomatic Struggle for East Timor* (Berto Wedhatama, Jakarta, 2006) he explained to *New York Times* reporter Jane Perlez that the title came from a remark once made to a Portuguese journalist who had asked him how he felt 'about the international stigma over East Timor'. He told her that he had replied that it was 'only as bothersome as a pebble in the shoe'. He then enlarged on the topic, saying that in retrospect 'in its final years, the East Timor problem was no longer a mere pebble in the shoe but had become a veritable boulder, dragging down Indonesia's international reputation to one of its lowest points'. Mr Alatas died in 2008. (Jane Perlez, A Book About East Timor Jabs Indonesia's Conscience', *New York Times* 17 August 2006.
18 C.R. Boxer, 'Portuguese Timor: A Rough Island History', *History Today*, Vol. X (1960), pp. 350–352
19 Ibid, p. 354.
20 Not his real name.
21 Its British name had been the HMS *Gurkha*.

22 http://meteorshowersonline.com/geminids/html downloaded 9 February 2010

23 Not his real name.

24 José Mattoso, *A Dignidade: Konis Santana e a Resistância Timorense*, Fundação Mário Soares, Lisboa, 2005, p. 302:

> Paira ainda um certo mistério sobre esta morte. Do ponto de vista histórico, não parece haver razôes para isso. Quem leu o seu correspondência sabe que esteve muitas vezes em perigo da vida durante os muitos combates que travou, ou ameacada por doenças graves, e que as condições em que vivia, fechado durante longos períodos num abrigo mal arejado, não eram saudáveis.

Prof. Mattoso's biography is the only extensive work on Nino Konis Santana, but was written entirely from documents provided by former resistance leaders post-1999. He never met Santana.

25 Mattoso, op. cit., p. 300:

> [Somotxo] escreveu um comunicado geral com data de 12 de Março, mas difundido mais tarde, em que declarava que Konis tinha morrido nas áreas de Ainaru, quando se diriga às regiões centrais em missão de reverificação das actividades politícas e militares. Este comunicado destinava-se a evitar que os Indonésios começassem a procurer o corpo, e dessam com o abrigo.

> [Somotxo] wrote a statement dated 12 March, but released later, in which he declared that Konis had died in the district of Ainaru, when he was marching to the central region to verify political and military activities. This statement was intended to avoid the Indonesians starting a search to find the body, and discovering the hideout.

Acknowledgements

Finding Santana was written with the help of many East Timorese people who supported my two 1994 journeys to the East Timor mountains to reach Nino Konis Santana. Some of them paid a high price when the second journey ended in disaster. Their story is told in these pages, and I am forever indebted to them.

They include Hernani Coelho da Silva, Avelino Coelho da Silva, Tomé Jeronimo, Rui Lourenço, Nuno Fernandes, José Reis, Natalino Coelho da Silva, Benvinda Rodrigues, Adolfo Belo, António Pinto Gouveia, Talofo, Hatta, Lulik, Father Domingos Soares, the late Father Hilário Madeira, the Arranhado family and a network of other resistance people too numerous to mention.

I am indebted to Xanana Kay Rala Gusmão for the interview he recorded and sent to me from Cipinang prison, Jakarta.

Malla Nunn was the brave anchor for the second, ill-fated, Timor journey, whose presence of mind at the catch-cry 'Auntie's sick!' allowed her to depart Indonesia coolly and minimise damage to the expedition.

Most of this book was written in one sitting over three weeks in 2004 at Varuna, The Writer's House, in Australia's Blue Mountains town of Katoomba. It resulted from the award of the Eric Dark Fellowship for a non-fiction manuscript of outstanding quality in social, historical or political writing.

My good friend Judy McLean of Katoomba not only

extracted me from danger in Indonesia in 1994 but provided extra-curricular hospitality during the writing of this manuscript at Varuna a decade later.

Richard Brown and Alex Butler also provided hospitality at their Anglesea retreat, a perfect setting to write.

Varuna's Peter Bishop always believed in the quality of this work and his encouragement and advocacy was determinant in its eventual publication.

Dr Jill Golden was another important advocate who helped bring the work to Wakefield Press and introduce me to publisher Michael Bollen.

Thanks to Prof. Jeri Kroll for inviting me to read extracts from the work at Flinders University's 'Writers and Their World' series, its first public airing.

My thanks to Dr Mark Williams for his detailed assessment of the manuscript and to Kevin Sherlock for his preparation of an index of a quality characteristic of East Timor's foremost bibliographer.

I am grateful to the staff of the Northern Territory Library who supported me during the final editing of the manuscript.

Dr John Cooper helped to keep me sane during this book's creation and kindly gave permission to quote material relating to my first sessions with him and the supervised *in vivo* consultations in Dili with Benvinda Rodrigues and Adolfo Belo. These were mediated in the East Timor capital by Dona Mira Martins da Silva, director of the mental health organisation PRADET, who also has my gratitude.

Thanks to Cathy Molnar for conducting the Lospalos photo run, even though its results weren't quite as we'd hoped, and to my former Lisbon colleague Marion Kaplan, who edited some of the photos from her home in southern France.

My agent John Stephen Timlin gave wise advice and support and I am indebted to Michael Bollen, Stephanie

Johnston, Ryan Paine and all at Wakefield Press for backing this book and bringing it to fruition.

This work is a memoir, based on diaries, reflecting the author's personal view of people and events. Any perceived misrepresentation of these is entirely my responsibility.

Index

Wakefield Press is an independent publishing and distribution company based in Adelaide, South Australia. We love good stories and publish beautiful books. To see our full range of titles, please visit our website at www.wakefieldpress.com.au.